T0323301

DESTRUCTIVE LEADERSHIP IN THE WORKPLACE & ITS CONSEQUENCES

SAGE SWIFTS SERIES

The **SAGE SWIFTS** series showcases the best of social science research that has the potential to influence public policy and practice, resulting in positive social change. We strongly believe that the social sciences are uniquely positioned to make this impact and thus benefit society in a myriad of ways.

SAGE SWIFTS celebrate and support the impact of quality empirical work that provides a provocative intervention into current debates, helping society to meet critical challenges going forward.

TITLES IN THE SERIES INCLUDE:

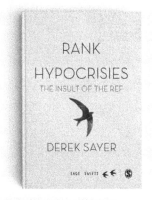

RANK HYPOCRISIES
THE INSULT OF THE REF
DEREK SAYER

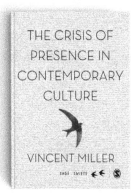

THE CRISIS OF PRESENCE IN CONTEMPORARY CULTURE
VINCENT MILLER

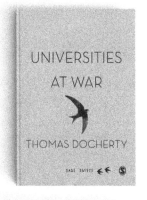

UNIVERSITIES AT WAR
THOMAS DOCHERTY

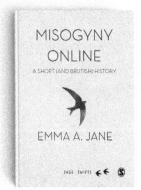

MISOGYNY ONLINE
A SHORT (AND BRUTISH) HISTORY
EMMA A. JANE

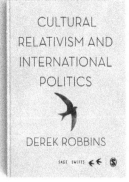

CULTURAL RELATIVISM AND INTERNATIONAL POLITICS
DEREK ROBBINS

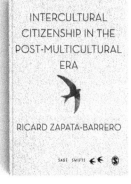

INTERCULTURAL CITIZENSHIP IN THE POST-MULTICULTURAL ERA
RICARD ZAPATA-BARRERO

DESTRUCTIVE LEADERSHIP IN THE WORKPLACE & ITS CONSEQUENCES

TRANSLATING THEORY & RESEARCH INTO EVIDENCE-BASED PRACTICE

VICKI WEBSTER
PAULA BROUGH

SAGE SWIFTS

SAGE

Los Angeles | London | New Delhi
Singapore | Washington DC | Melbourne

Los Angeles | London | New Delhi
Singapore | Washington DC | Melbourne

SAGE Publications Ltd
1 Oliver's Yard
55 City Road
London EC1Y 1SP

SAGE Publications Inc.
2455 Teller Road
Thousand Oaks, California 91320

SAGE Publications India Pvt Ltd
B 1/I 1 Mohan Cooperative Industrial Area
Mathura Road
New Delhi 110 044

SAGE Publications Asia-Pacific Pte Ltd
3 Church Street
#10-04 Samsung Hub
Singapore 049483

Editor: Donna Goddard
Assistant editor: Esmé Carter
Production editor: Sushant Nailwal
Copyeditor: Sunrise Setting
Proofreader: Sunrise Setting
Indexer: Sunrise Setting
Marketing manager: Camille Richmond
Cover design: Wendy Scott
Typeset by C&M Digitals (P) Ltd, Chennai, India

Library of Congress Control Number: 2021945980

British Library Cataloguing in Publication data

A catalogue record for this book is available from the British Library

ISBN 978-1-5297-2416-5
eISBN 978-1-5297-6570-0

CONTENTS

LIST OF FIGURES AND TABLES

ABOUT THE AUTHORS

Vicki Webster is Founder and Director of Incisive Leaders. Vicki is a Leadership Specialist, Executive Coach and Organisational Psychologist. Vicki completed her research PhD on the dark side of leadership and its impact on followers in 2016. She has considerable practical experience in leadership assessment, design and implementation of leadership development programmes and design and implementation of interventions to protect organisations and employees from the effects of destructive leadership. Vicki is keen to share evidence-based strategies with as many researchers, managers and practitioners as possible, to give them the tools to mitigate the impact of destructive leadership in organisations. Results of Vicki's research and organisational programmes have been published in a range of forums: she is co-author of 'Assisting organisations to deal effectively with toxic leadership in the workplace', *InPsych* (2015), 'Fight, flight or freeze: Common responses for follower coping with toxic leadership', *Stress & Health* (2016), 'Toxic boss at work', *The Conversation* (2015), and *How to get ahead without murdering your boss: Six simple steps to actively manage your career* (2010).

Paula Brough is a Professor of Organisational Psychology and Director of the Centre for Work, Organisation and Wellbeing at Griffith University in Brisbane, Australia. Paula's primary research and teaching areas are occupational stress and coping, employee mental health and wellbeing, work engagement, work–life balance, workplace conflict (bullying, harassment, toxic leadership) and the psychosocial work environment. Paula assesses how work environments can be improved via job redesign, supportive leadership practices and enhanced equity to improve employee health, work commitment and productivity. Paula has authored over 60 industry reports and over 150 journal articles and book chapters, and has produced nine scholarly books based on her research. Paula is an Associate Editor of *Work & Stress* and is Board Member of the *Journal of Organizational Behaviour*, *International Journal of Stress Management* and the *BPS Work-Life Balance Bulletin*. Paula is also a Fellow of the European Academy of Occupational Health Psychology and a Fellow of the Asia Pacific Academy for Psychosocial Factors at Work.

SECTION I

DESTRUCTIVE LEADERSHIP AND ITS IMPACT

I

INTRODUCTION

CHAPTER OVERVIEW

Over the past two decades, considerable research has investigated the phenomenon of destructive leadership, also described as abusive supervision, aversive
leadership, the dark side of leadership, derailing leadership, toxic leadership,
tyrannical leadership and the dark triad of leadership. This book discusses this
body of research of destructive leadership in organisations from both leader
and follower perspectives and identifies the systems and organisational contexts that enable destructive leadership behaviours to flourish. While there has
been significant research into the consequences of destructive leadership and
the organisational responses to it, there has been limited investigation of
its antecedents and how best to protect targets from the psychological, emotional and physical harm caused by destructive leadership. This first chapter
provides an overview of the destructive leadership literature and the key topics
discussed in each chapter of this book.

DESTRUCTIVE LEADERSHIP

Leaders who achieve great things in one domain, such as Steve Jobs, Harvey
Weinstein and Margaret Thatcher, can demonstrate their dark side by engaging in behaviours that cause harm. Across the globe we hear of leaders abusing
their political power. For example, the media is currently reporting on the toxic
culture created by the Sony CEO for over 30 years. This book explores the
mechanisms by which leaders engage in destructive leadership behaviours,
how they 'get away with it' and why it can take so long to remove them from
positions of power.

   Over the past two decades, scholarly attention has increasingly discussed
the harmful behaviours displayed by some organisational managers and leaders.

This increase in attention was expedited by a special edition of *Leadership Quarterly* (Tierney & Tepper, 2007) dedicated to the topic of *destructive leadership*. This phenomenon has subsequently been studied under the research stream of destructive leadership, which includes the comparable research terms of 'abusive supervision', 'the dark side of leadership', 'aversive', 'despotic', 'unethical', 'toxic' and 'tyrannical' leadership. The phenomenon of destructive leadership has predominantly been approached from two perspectives. First, the *leader-centric* approach focused on leaders' destructive characteristics and behaviours. Second, a *follower-centric* approach, led by the abusive supervision literature, focused on the subjective assessment made by subordinates in response to sustained abuse by their leader. There has been notable increased interest in how followers enact their own role in the leadership relationship – that is, the way they communicate with the leader, comply with their instructions and respond to their behaviour. However, social constructions of leadership and/or followership are directly informed by the context in which the leader/follower dyad interaction occurs. Research attention has thus also considered the situational contexts that provide an ideal environment for destructive leadership to flourish, such as times of instability, social or economic threat and the absence of checks and balances for power and control.

In their experiences, the authors have directly observed the negative effects destructive leadership has on individuals' wellbeing. Despite the conceptual and theory building that destructive leadership research has conducted to date, there remains a lack of empirical studies to inform evidence-based practice on how best to address this issue in practical terms. Additionally, much of the useful research published in academic journals is difficult for practitioners to readily access. The aim of this book, therefore, is to provide an informed bridge between academic research and organisational practice, focusing on the evidence-based interventions designed to address destructive leadership and its impact within workplaces. For the purposes of this book, we use the term 'destructive leadership' to include all forms of leadership that cause harm to followers. Thus, the terms 'destructive leadership', 'toxic leadership' and 'abusive supervision' are used interchangeably throughout this book, depending on the focus of the research discussed. Similarly, unless specifically designated, the multiple terms employed to describe followers, 'workers', 'employees', 'subordinates' or 'targets of destructive leadership', are also employed interchangeably throughout this book.

To assist you in navigating this book, we summarise here the key topics discussed in each chapter. The first eight chapters set the context for much of the research conducted on destructive leadership. In Chapter 2, we provide a comprehensive review of the individual, group and organisational factors that enable destructive leadership to exist and discuss the complexity organisations face when attempting to prevent or address this issue. Chapter 3 discusses the key antecedents of destructive leadership identified in the research literature, including the contributions of a lack of self-awareness and failure of self-management and of leaders engaging in harmful behaviours. In Chapter 4, we identify the common consequences of destructive leadership, for the leaders themselves, their targets, teams and organisations. In Chapter 5, we discuss the relevant organisational cultural factors that provide a conducive environment for the prevalence of destructive leadership. In Chapter 6, we address the issue of organisational silence and inaction in the face of destructive leadership. Chapter 6 also discusses the common reasons why organisations, managers and employees may turn a blind eye to destructive leadership behaviours. In Chapter 7, we discuss the consequences of destructive leadership for individuals, targets and employees, including short- and long-term psychological, emotional, physical and career harm. We describe the factors that influence the leader's perception of their target and the target characteristics that may lead to an increase or decrease in abuse. Finally, in Chapter 8, we review the research describing the vulnerabilities of targets of destructive leadership, the theoretical explanations for how targets identify, respond to and cope with destructive leadership behaviours and the effectiveness of the coping strategies they choose to employ.

The second section of the book focuses on the efficacy of organisational interventions in addressing destructive leadership. In Chapter 9, we summarise the current academic and business assessment tools and tactics for identifying destructive leadership, including an assessment of the advantages and disadvantages of each measure. Chapter 9 also describes current trends and positive and negative examples of specific workplace interventions. In Chapter 10, we describe the key strategies and components included in effective leadership development programmes, which aim to reduce the prevalence of destructive leadership in existing and future leaders. We also identify activities to enhance self-awareness of blind spots and self-management to reduce impulsivity. In Chapter 11, we provide guidance on strategies to protect employees, including a discussion of the key design principles and common difficulties in designing and implementing interventions to help protect targets/followers from the harm of destructive leadership. Chapter 12 focuses on the common organisational responses to complaints of destructive leadership, and we consider alternative interventions, such as workplace conferencing (a form of restorative justice), and how those interventions compare with typical investigative and mediation strategies. Finally, in Chapter 13, we summarise the key learnings and practical implications identified by this book. We also consider emerging areas of organisational behavioural research that are increasingly relevant to destructive leadership research.

In summary, this book provides reviews of the principal theories, research studies and organisational practices in relation to the occurrence and exposure of destructive leadership and thus serves as a useful reference source for both organisational researchers and practitioners. This book also contributes to the growing research field of destructive leadership, combining theory and practice to inform how organisations and individuals can best respond to destructive leadership behaviours.

2

DESTRUCTIVE LEADERSHIP AS A WICKED PROBLEM

CHAPTER OVERVIEW

A sustained demonstration of destructive leadership behaviours is associated with numerous harmful outcomes, primarily the serious psychological and emotional distress for impacted employees. Unfortunately, in response, many organisational reactions fall short of providing an appropriate duty of care to their employees. Destructive leadership can be viewed as a 'wicked problem' because there is no single solution to the problem. This chapter discusses the key relationships between destructive leaders, susceptible followers and the contextual environments that allow destructive leadership to flourish in organisations.

DESTRUCTIVE LEADERSHIP AS A WICKED PROBLEM

Imagine. Imagine that as the alarm goes off, you awake with a sense of dread. Your stomach is churning. Waves of nausea overwhelm you. You feel the beginnings of a headache. The last thing you want to do is go to work and face them. As soon as you walk into work, you can hear them yelling abuse at one of your colleagues. Last week they accepted public praise for the excellent work they had done on a very important project, knowing full well it was your work. Your colleagues avoid your eye as you walk by. They treat you as if you have an infectious disease – you are out of favour and they want nothing to do with you. 'Chris, you idiot, get yourself in here!' Red in the face, eyes bulging. Not a good sign, but you daren't refuse. You've raised your concerns, and nothing has been done. You just don't know how much longer you can take this.

Traditionally, organisational leadership research adopted the approach that all leaders are inherently good and ethical. The scenario described above, which clearly suggests otherwise, is derived from the responses of those who had experienced chronic destructive leadership, collected within one of the author's research studies. Kellerman, a political scientist, also challenged this view of leaders as being 'inherently good and ethical':

> In spite of all the work on leadership that assumes it by definition to be good... we exercise power, authority and influence in ways that do harm. This harm is not necessarily deliberate. It can be the result of carelessness or neglect. But this does not make it less injurious and, in some cases, calamitous. (Kellerman, 2004, p. xiii)

Some research regards *destructive leadership* as an oxymoron, asserting leadership is, by definition, a positive force. However, other research has demonstrated that it is equally important to understand *why* people and organisations tolerate destructive leaders (Kellerman, 2004; Lipman-Blumen, 2005). Kellerman (2004) noted that a focus on the 'bright' or 'light' side of leadership resulted in little attention being paid to the followership of 'bad' leaders, whether it be in the political arena, the community or business. Influential leaders who have subsequently been labelled evil, despotic dictators have been extraordinarily successful in retaining large numbers of followers who adopted their purpose, values, ideas and directives (McNeill, 2020).

> *Imagine. You are just leaving your doctor's office with the forms signed so you can take sick leave from work, and lodge a stress claim against your employer, if you choose to. You have insomnia, a skin rash that won't go away, have been diagnosed with irritable bowel syndrome and your hair is coming out by the handful. You vacillate between bursts of anger and irritability and becoming teary at the most inconvenient and embarrassing times. Your doctor has referred you to a psychologist. The diagnosis is that all your symptoms have been caused by stress at work. You feel ashamed that you've let your boss get to you to the point it has come to this. If you lose your job, you don't know how you are going to pay the mortgage.*

Destructive leadership produces a range of negative consequences for leaders, individual followers and organisations, including, for example, leader derailment, reduced performance, reduced wellbeing, reduced employee satisfaction and commitment, increased absenteeism, unwanted turnover and high numbers of formal occupational stress claims arising from psychological distress (Schyns & Schilling, 2013; Tepper, 2000, 2007). Common employee negative psychological outcomes caused by destructive leadership include reduced self-esteem, feelings of threat to security, distress at unjust treatment, disengagement and burnout (Pelletier, 2010; Tepper, 2000). In addition, perceptions of abusive treatment by a leader may lead to retaliatory responses by followers (Tepper, 2007). This chapter explores this 'wicked problem' by reviewing the relevant destructive leadership research, describing the key types of destructive leaders identified within the research literature and summarising the common organisational responses to the occurrence of destructive leadership.

DESTRUCTIVE LEADERSHIP RESEARCH

The complex phenomenon of destructive leadership, including its antecedents and enablers, indicates this type of leadership is best considered as a 'wicked problem'. A wicked problem is a problem that is difficult or impossible to solve because of incomplete, contradictory and changing requirements that are difficult to recognise and that has no single solution (Hoffren & Laulainen, 2018). Given the severity of consequences experienced by many targets of destructive leadership, it is important for effective dialogue to occur between leadership researchers and practitioners in order to achieve an improved understanding of the systemic causes of destructive leadership and the most effective methods to prevent or address its impacts.

Leadership research can be conceptualised on a continuum, from the anchor point of constructive leadership through to destructive leadership (see Figure 2.1). Destructive leadership research consists of multiple terms, overlapping definitions, numerous behavioural dimensions and several categories of destructive leaders (Einarsen, Aasland & Skogstad, 2007; Martinko, Harvey, Brees & Mackey, 2013). Thus, for example, diverse destructive leadership research streams have variously described it as incompetent and unethical leadership (Conger, 1990; Kellerman, 2004), personalised charismatic leadership (House & Howell, 1992), petty tyranny (Ashforth, 1994), abusive supervision (Tepper, 2000), aversive leadership (Bligh, Kohles, Pearce, Justin & Stovall, 2007), toxic leadership (Lipman-Blumen, 2005), leader bullying (Ferris, Zinko, Brouer, Buckley & Harvey, 2007), despotic leadership (De Hoogh & Den Hartog, 2008) and the dark side of laissez-faire leadership (Burns, 2021; Skogstad, Einarsen, Torsheim, Aasland & Hetland, 2007).

Constructive leadership
Bright side of leadership
(values-based leadership)

- Authentic leadership
- Charismatic leadership
- Ethical leadership
- Responsible leadership
- Servant leadership
- Spiritual leadership
- Transformational leadership

Derailed leadership
Dark side of leadership
(strengths in extreme)

Strengths overused, e.g.:
- Extreme self-confidence becomes arrogance
- Extreme assertiveness becomes intimidation
- Extreme competitiveness becomes manipulation
- Extreme affiliation becomes passive-aggressiveness
- Extreme need for control becomes micromanaging

Negative traits not addressed, e.g.:
- Low emotional control leads to extreme moods, unpredictability and volatility

Destructive leadership
Dark side of leadership
(harm to individuals and organisations)

- Abusive supervision
- Aversive leadership
- Dark side charismatic
- Dark side transformational
- Dark side authentic
- Laissez-faire leadership
- Machiavellian leadership
- Narcissistic leadership
- Organisational psychopaths/sociopaths (subclinical)
- Toxic leadership
- Tyrannical leadership
- Unethical leadership

Leader self-regulation

Negative affectivity and poor leader self-regulation

Follower courage, influence and voice

Follower fear, blind obedience, silence and compliance

Figure 2.1   Conceptual model of the interaction of leadership style, leader self-regulation and followership.

Table 2.1 also summarises the range of definitions, destructive leadership behaviours and categories of destructive leaders that can be drawn from the key research literature. The destructive leadership research literature falls under four main themes: *leader derailment, abusive supervision, toxic leadership* and *the dark triad of leadership*.

Table 2.1   Summary of destructive leadership definitions and focus.

Author	Construct	Definition	Focus of research
Lombardo et al. (1988)	Leader derailment	Plateaued, demoted or fired below the level of anticipated achievement or reaching that level only to fail unexpectedly.	Career derailment; harm to the leader.
Schmit et al. (2000)	Leader derailment	The tendency to use quasi-leadership tactics or to engage in various behaviours that may prove successful in changing others behaviour in the short term, but ultimately cause the leader to fail or lose support of those around him or her.	Harm caused to followers: • Derailing personality traits (GPI).
Hogan and Hogan (2001)	Leader derailment	Managerial incompetence due to a dysfunctional disposition.	Harm caused to followers: • Derailing personality traits (HDS).
Tepper (2000)	Abusive supervision	A sustained display of hostile verbal and nonverbal behaviours, excluding physical contact.	Harm caused to followers: • Behaviours perceived as abusive by followers.
Lipman-Blumen (2005)	Toxic leadership	Engaging in numerous destructive behaviours and exhibiting certain dysfunctional personal characteristics. To be toxic, these behaviours and qualities of character must inflict some reasonably serious and enduring harm on their followers and their organisations.	Harm caused to followers and organisations: • Dysfunctional personality characteristics; • Destructive behaviours.

(Continued)

Table 2.1   (Continued)

Author	Construct	Definition	Focus of research
Einarsen et al. (2007)	Destructive leadership	The systematic and repeated behaviour by a leader, supervisor or manager that violates the legitimate interest of the organisation by undermining and/or sabotaging the organisation's goals, tasks, resources and effectiveness and/or the motivation, wellbeing or job satisfaction of subordinates.	Harm caused to the organisation and followers: • Tyrannical leadership; • Derailed leadership; • Supportive – disloyal; • Constructive.
Krasikova et al. (2013)	Destructive leadership	Volitional behaviour by a leader that can harm or intends to harm a leader's organisation and/or followers by (a) encouraging followers to pursue goals that contravene the legitimate interests of the organisation and/or (b) employing a leadership style that involves the use of harmful methods of influence with followers, regardless of justifications for such behaviour.	Harm caused to the organisation and followers.
Schyns and Schilling (2013)	Destructive leadership	A process in which over a longer period of time the activities, experiences and/or relationships of an individual or the members of a group are repeatedly influenced by their supervisor in a way that is perceived as hostile and/or obstructive.	Harm caused to followers.

GPI – Global Personality Inventory

HDS – Hogan Development Survey

The phenomenon of destructive leadership has predominantly been studied from two perspectives. First, the *leader-centric* approach focuses on leaders' destructive characteristics, motivations and behaviours (Einarsen et al., 2007;

Brandebo & Alvinius, 2019; Krasikova, Green & LeBreton, 2013; Schyns & Hansborough, 2010). As leader-centric approaches have been criticised for being too one-sided, interest has grown in how followers enact their own role in the leadership relationship, with a focus on their *followership* (e.g., the way they communicate with the leader, comply with their instructions and respond to their behaviour; Barbuto, 2000; Kellerman, 2008; Uhl-Bien, Riggio, Lowe & Carsten, 2014). Second, a *follower-centric* approach, led by the abusive supervision literature, has focused on the subjective assessment that subordinates make of a sustained display of hostile verbal and nonverbal behaviours (Martinko et al., 2013; Tepper, 2007). Thus, theoretical explanations of destructive leadership have expanded to consider factors external to a leader's direct role. Specifically, research has investigated both the role and interaction of leaders' and followers' personality characteristics, leaders' and followers' motivations and how these are activated by environmental context and opportunity (Krasikova et al., 2013; Mulvey & Padilla, 2010; Padilla, Hogan & Kaiser, 2007).

Three primary domains of destructive leadership were proposed by both Padilla et al. (2007) and Thoroughgood, Padilla, Hunter and Tate (2012). In the first domain, an individual leader will have a predisposition, through one or more of their personality trait characteristics, to default to dark side leadership behaviours, in combination with a motivation to achieve their own agenda, even at the expense of others. Padilla et al. (2007) identified five key components of this type of destructive leadership (see Table 2.2), highlighting the characteristics of destructive leaders, their focus on self-interest (personalised power) and how they cause harm to both individuals and organisations.

Table 2.2   Five features of destructive leadership.

1. Destructive leadership is seldom absolutely or entirely destructive: there are both good and bad results in most leadership situations.
2. The process of destructive leadership involves dominance, coercion, and manipulation rather than influence, persuasion, and commitment.
3. The process of destructive leadership has a selfish orientation; it is focused more on the leader's needs than the needs of the larger social group.
4. The effects of destructive leadership are outcomes that compromise the quality of life for constituents and detract from the organisation's main purposes.
5. Destructive organisational outcomes are not exclusively the result of destructive leaders but are also products of susceptible followers and conducive environments.

Source: Padilla et al. (2007, p. 179).

In the second domain, followers comply with destructive leaders' demands and may even support and promote destructive leadership. Padilla et al. (2007) defined two types of susceptible followers: *conformers*, who lack a clearly defined self-concept and comply with destructive leaders out of fear, primarily to minimise their personal consequences of non-compliance, and *colluders*, who may share the leader's values and actively participate in the destructive leader's agenda in order to seek personal gain through their association with the leader.

Finally, in the third domain, the environment or context also allows destructive leadership behaviours to occur and to be tolerated, and we discuss in detail how organisational cultures contribute to destructive leadership in Chapter 5. Social constructions of leadership and/or followership are informed by the context in which the leader/follower dyad interaction occurs (Brandebo & Alvinius, 2019; van Knippenberg, 2012). Situational influences include organisations that foster low control and high co-operation, and large bureaucracies with high power-distance between managers and employees. Organisational instability (e.g., periods of radical change) and perceived threat (e.g., social or economic threats and crises) create environments where more assertive, autocratic leadership may be tolerated (Brandebo, 2020). Cultural values and norms (e.g., organisational cultures that endorse the avoidance of uncertainty and collectivism, as opposed to individualism, or fail to provide an ethical climate – which we specifically discuss in Chapter 6) also influence whether destructive leadership will be tolerated. Similarly, an absence of appropriate checks and balances of power and control by an organisation, which results in a concentration of power in the leader, is another type of organisational context that enables destructive leadership behaviours to occur (Mulvey & Padilla, 2010; O'Boyle & Forsyth, 2012; Padilla et al., 2007; Tepper, 2007). These three domains represent the key inter-relationships between destructive leadership, taxonomies of susceptible followers and the contextual environments that enable destructive leadership to flourish in organisations.

DESTRUCTIVE LEADERS

Destructive leadership is demonstrated by a pattern of behaviour by a leader that sabotages or undermines the achievement of subordinates and/or organisations by focusing purely on the leader's self-interest. In an attempt to integrate the destructive leadership literature, Einarsen et al. (2007) developed a model to describe the difference between constructive and destructive leadership, based on whether the leader behaviour benefited individuals and the organisation or caused them harm. Their model has two basic dimensions: *subordinate-oriented behaviours* and *organisation-oriented behaviours*. Anti-subordinate behaviours, such as harassment and mistreatment, violate the organisation's interests by sabotaging the motivation and wellbeing of subordinates. Of specific interest here are the two dimensions concerned with anti-subordinate behaviour: *derailed leadership dimension* (anti-subordinate and anti-organisation), such as manipulating subordinates while simultaneously defrauding the organisation, and the *tyrannical leadership dimension* (anti-subordinate and pro-organisation), such as humiliating or belittling a subordinate in order to complete a task or project.

Leader derailment or situational strengths?

Leader derailment has been defined as either career derailment (McCall & Lombardo, 1983) or as an overuse of strengths (Benson & Campbell, 2007; Kaiser & Hogan, 2011). Leader career derailment is a combination of an inability to develop or adapt (e.g., inability to learn from mistakes or from direct feedback) and a lack of important characteristics or abilities to succeed (e.g., low levels of personality traits such as agreeableness, inability to build effective working relations). The common causes of leader career derailment identified within the literature include adopting an insensitive, abrasive or bullying style; adopting an autocratic, controlling style; displaying aloofness, arrogance or self-centred ambition; being emotionally volatile; failing to listen to a contrary point of view or heed conflicting information; and failing to constructively face an obvious problem (Baker et al., 2018; Judge, Piccolo & Kolsaka, 2009; Williams, Campell, McCartney & Gooding, 2013).

The 'strengths in extreme' explanation for leader derailment proposes that there is an optimal level of personality traits. This trait approach explains negative leadership behaviours principally in terms of the occurrence of extreme bright side or dark side personality traits predisposing the leader to exhibit inappropriate or harmful behaviours, which in turn lead to leader derailment. Interestingly, an *excessive* level of bright side traits is associated with derailing leadership behaviours, while exhibiting a *moderate* level of dark side tendencies can be beneficial to leadership success (Furnham, Trickey & Hyde, 2012; Judge et al., 2009; Kaiser, LeBreton & Hogan, 2015). Destructive leadership theorists propose that behaviour towards subordinates and the organisation that departs from constructive leadership behaviour ultimately causes the leader to fail (Einarsen et al., 2007).

Dysfunctional traits and behaviours tend to be especially demonstrated in difficult and stressful contexts, when success is seen as crucial, when there are time and workload pressures and when a leader's personal and psychological resources are depleted (Benson & Campbell, 2007; Byrne et al., 2014). Although leaders may be well intentioned and generally focused on achieving individual, team or organisational objectives, if they have a preference to employ these derailing behaviours to achieve their goals, it will hinder their effectiveness over time, through a loss of support from followers and peers. The difference between leaders who leverage situational strengths and those who derail is commonly due to their ability to control their impulsivity, regulate their actions and utilise their characteristics in situations that are appropriate (Collins & Jackson, 2015; Furnham et al., 2012; Judge et al., 2009; Wang, Sinclair & Deese, 2010). There is evidence that derailing managers can change their adverse behaviours, but this typically requires more intensive training and coaching than is commonly found in traditional organisational leadership development programmes (Sandler, 2012).

This idea that leaders need a balance between their dark side and bright side traits creates a paradox for the concept of authentic leadership. Thus, the need to regulate and restrain a leader's natural inclinations, such as taking centre stage or being too determined and honest, may go against the nature of that leader's true self (Nyberg & Sveningsson, 2014). Effective leaders must, therefore, reconcile the need to be true to themselves with the need to be aware of how their behaviour will be perceived by others. In turn, how their behaviour is perceived by others is based on their followers' implicit prototypes of a good/bad leader within the context of social norms (Hansbrough & Schyns, 2010). One definition of destructive leadership that is based on followers' perceptions is abusive supervision.

Abusive supervision

Research on abusive supervision has focused on sustained displays of a supervisor's hostility (non-physical), as determined by subordinates' assessments, based on their observations of a supervisor's behaviour. Abusive supervision includes behaviours such as yelling, ridicule, rudeness, breaking promises, invading privacy, lying and using the silent treatment (Tepper, 2000). Supervisors perpetrate abusive behaviour for a purpose – for example, to increase performance or reduce mistakes. However, it is not necessary for the supervisor to intend to cause harm for their behaviour to be included in this category. Supervisors who score low in agreeableness (more argumentative, hostile and conflictive) and score high in neuroticism (experiencing greater anger, frustration and impulsiveness) are more likely to be abusive. However, there is limited research specifically on the personality traits of supervisors that subordinates perceive as abusive, with the exception of supervisors with psychopathic traits, who are reported to be particularly abusive (Boddy, 2011; Martinko et al., 2013). Research assessing the antecedents of abusive supervision reports that supervisors who abuse subordinates primarily target their hostility on those who appear to be weak, vulnerable and unwilling or unable to defend themselves (Tepper, Duffy, Henle & Lambert, 2006). Supervisors who had themselves experienced unfavourable interpersonal treatment from their manager, and who embraced dominance and control as legitimate forms of leadership, were also more abusive towards subordinates (Aryee, Chen, Sun & Debrah, 2007; Schyns & Schilling, 2013). A second definition of destructive leadership that is based on followers' perceptions is toxic leadership.

Toxic leadership

Toxic leadership is determined by evaluating the consequences of a leader's behaviour, based on their followers' perceptions and attributions (Lipman-Blumen, 2005; Milosevic, Maric & Lončar, 2020). Leaders are considered toxic when they inflict serious and enduring harm on their constituents by using influence tactics that are extremely hard and/or malicious, and when their actions result in long-lasting physical, emotional or psychological harm to followers. Pelletier (2010) conducted an exploratory study with 200 US employees to identify a typology of toxic leader behavioural characteristics. These were categorised under eight behavioural dimensions: (a) attacking followers' self-esteem (e.g., ridiculing and mocking), (b) divisiveness (e.g., pitting one employee against another), (c) social exclusion (e.g., excluding individuals from social functions), (d) promoting inequity (e.g., exhibiting favouritism), (e) abusiveness (e.g., tantrums, yelling), (f) threatening followers' security (e.g., using physical acts of aggression), (g) lack of integrity (e.g., being deceptive) and (h) laissez-faire leadership style (e.g., failing to respond when employees voiced concerns). These eight dimensions have also been validated by other researchers (e.g., Heppell, 2011; Martinko et al., 2013; Skogstad et al., 2007).

The dark triad: Narcissism, Machiavellianism and psychopathy

One of the most serious categories of destructive leadership is the *dark triad*: narcissism, Machiavellianism and subclinical psychopathy (Boddy, 2015; Furnham, Richards & Paulhus, 2013; Furtner, Maran & Rauthmann, 2017).

Individuals with these dark triad traits may be promoted into leadership roles due to their ability to present a positive impression. They may even lie about their qualifications and achievements to enhance their attractiveness as a candidate. They are also likely to be promoted if they have the capability to suppress the damaging behaviours associated with these syndromes. Once in positions of authority, they may be considered successful if these traits are consistent with the demands of their management/executive role, as long as they are able to control their impulsivity and anti-social tendencies. However, these personality traits often ensure that this type of leader demonstrates inadequate performance and increased counterproductive work behaviours (O'Boyle & Forsyth, 2012). These leaders are also difficult to manage and are not amenable to changing their behaviour, as their primary motivations are personal power and self-interest.

The literature on *narcissism* also examines the bright side of leadership and authority (charisma and vision), the maladaptive aspects of narcissism (grandiose exhibitionism) and the dark side of this characteristic (exploitativeness and entitlement) (Campbell, Hoffman, Campbell & Marchisio, 2011; Grijalva, Harms, Newman, Gaddis & Fraley, 2015; Grijalva & Newman, 2015; House & Howell, 1992; Rosenthal & Pittinsky, 2006). Narcissistic individuals typically have an inflated view of themselves and their abilities, feel entitled to excessive rewards and recognition and seek out roles that provide them with power and influence. Extreme levels of narcissistic self-importance and arrogance can lead to demonstrations of intense desire to compete, high levels of distrust (constantly on the lookout for enemies), sensitivity to criticism that threatens self-image, lack of empathy and a high level of risk-taking, without listening to words of caution or advice from others. Narcissistic leaders are often abrasive and aggressive with those who attempt to resist or oppose them. While these types of leaders seek the admiration and adulation of others, they also risk isolating themselves at the very moment of their success, because narcissistic relationships contain low levels of empathy and emotional intimacy. Narcissistic leaders typically have numerous shallow relationships that can range from exciting and engaging to manipulative and exploitative (Braun, 2016; Campbell et al., 2011; Furtner, Rauthmann & Sachse, 2011; Leary & Ashman, 2018; Maccoby, 2007).

Machiavellian leaders have a propensity to distrust others, engage in amoral manipulation, seek to control others and seek status for themselves (e.g., personalised power). While Machiavellian leaders may be charismatic, they are typically unsupportive and inconsiderate of others, often engaging in political influencing tactics such as strategic self-disclosure, ingratiation and intimidation

(Dahling, Whitaker & Levy, 2009). Machiavellian leaders overall tend to be self-promoters, who behave in a cold, manipulative fashion for their own purposes (Belschak, Muhammad & Den Hartog, 2018; Furtner et al., 2017; Keng, Feng & Li, 2018).

The concept of *organisational psychopaths* in the workplace (also referred to in the literature as corporate psychopaths or organisational sociopaths) was initiated by Babiak and Hare (2007) in their book *Snakes in suits*, and also by Clarke (2005) in his book *Working with monsters.* These authors provided definitions, examples and case studies describing the most negative aspects of the narcissistic and Machiavellian attributes demonstrated by organisational leaders. Since then, there has been ongoing research investigating the characteristics of organisational psychopaths (Babiak, Neumann & Hare, 2010; Boddy, 2015; Furtner et al., 2017). It is estimated that approximately 3–4% of individuals in higher-level positions in organisations exhibit subclinical psychopathy traits. There are several taxonomies of workplace psychopathy, but it has been usefully conceptualised to consist of affective and interpersonal traits of psychopathy (e.g., guiltlessness, lack of empathy, grandiosity, egocentricity and superficial charm), impulsivity, irresponsibility and a lack of behavioural controls (Furtner et al., 2011; Smith & Lilienfeld, 2013). Characteristics of subclinical psychopathic types of leaders include:

- manipulative organisational behaviours,
- unethical behaviours,
- intolerance (easily bored),
- unpredictable behaviours/shallow emotions,
- parasitic behaviours,
- failing to take responsibility for behaviours,
- intimidating/bullying, creating a culture of fear,
- seeking increased personal power and control,
- claiming credit for work they have not done,
- blaming others for things that go wrong,
- creating conflict between organisational members,
- deceit and deviousness, and
- charm/superficiality.

Despite the widely held view that psychopathy is invariably maladaptive, some researchers have argued that mild expressions of some of its characteristics (e.g., fearlessness and charm) can be useful in certain settings, such as entrepreneurial activities and in negotiating business dealings (Smith & Lilienfeld, 2013). However, due to the negative behaviours of these leaders, their lack of insight and the fear they instil in those around them, this is an extremely difficult area to research. Some theorists suggest that the only way to manage this type of leader is to remove them from the organisation 'like cutting out a cancer' (Babiak & Hare, 2007; Boddy, 2015; Clarke, 2005).

ORGANISATIONAL RESPONSES TO DESTRUCTIVE LEADERSHIP

The research literature repeatedly urges employers to treat their employees with respect and dignity, while also being focused on productivity and profits. The literature emphasises the importance of strong, ethical leadership, fair treatment and frequent, effective communication. In some countries, employers have a legal duty of care for both the physical and psychological wellbeing of their employees (Brough, Raper & Spedding, 2020). Mechanisms for employees to protect their rights include unions and equal employment laws (e.g., harassment, anti-discrimination and bullying legislation). However, destructive leadership remains prevalent and is even thriving in some toxic organisational cultures. The drive for corporations to maximise short-term profits, based on investor or shareholder influence and stock market pressure, provides an environment where the ends may be seen to justify the means. Public sector and not-for-profit organisations increasingly expect managers to find ways to raise revenue and reduce expenditure, especially in the context of the financial impact of the COVID-19 pandemic. As a result of this short-term focus on profits and financial sustainability, the workplace has become a place where employees are often treated badly and managers are rewarded for engaging in destructive behaviours (Daniel, 2020).

The best way to manage the risk of destructive leadership is to ensure that the proper procedures and processes are in place to minimise psychosocial risks to employees and to ensure high levels of employee health and wellbeing. Recommended organisational interventions to install checks and balances to guard against destructive leadership include organisational controls and sanctions, strong corporate governance, the setting of organisational norms and expectations regarding acceptable behaviour through an ethics code or code of conduct, the promoting of organisational values, whistle-blower policies, robust performance management and disciplinary policies and processes, leadership development programmes, team-building programmes to reduce inter-team and intra-team conflict and the provision of employee assistance programmes to counsel and support targets of destructive leaders (Dewe, 1994; Padilla et al., 2007; Wotruba, Chonko & Loe, 2001). However, we note that despite these measures, destructive leadership remains prevalent in many organisations.

Legal risk to organisations

There is no legislation that addresses destructive leadership by a manager as a discrete issue, with the exception of workplace bullying. The regulation of workplace bullying is covered by a number of legal frameworks, including workplace health and safety, workers' compensation, criminal law, anti-discrimination and industrial relations law. Legislation allows for the imposition of penalties to organisations being found in breach of the legislation or the provision of compensation to the target after the event. If an organisation chooses to dismiss an offending manager, the employer must be careful to ensure that the employee is made aware of the conduct that is not acceptable and the employee must be given an opportunity to rectify their conduct. It is essential that the employee be told that if they do not rectify their conduct, their contract may be terminated (Catanzariti & Egan, 2015).

Workplace health and safety legislation

Workplace health and safety legislation stipulates that employers have an obligation to ensure, as far as reasonably practicable, the health and safety, including psychological health, of their workers while they are at work (Brough et al., 2020). Similarly, workers are required to take reasonable care that their acts or omissions do not adversely affect other workers, and to comply with the health and safety requirements at the workplace. Once a complaint has been received, there may be an investigation into the workplace. If a breach is found, the regulator may issue a compliance notice or prosecute. Various criminal penalties apply to breaches of workplace health and safety laws and both individuals and organisations can be convicted (Catanzariti & Egan, 2015).

Anti-discrimination legislation

If the abusive behaviour, or the reason for the abuse, can be linked to a relevantly protected trait (i.e., gender, gender identity, sexual orientation, race, age, disability, religion or family responsibilities), then the target of the abuse may have a remedy pursuant to anti-discrimination legislation. Employer organisations may be exposed to legal risk in the form of an indirect discrimination claim. Indirect discrimination occurs when a person imposes a condition, requirement or practice that has the effect of disadvantaging an employee with a protected attribute (Catanzariti & Egan, 2015). Managers often have access to workers' employment files, which may include information on a protected attribute. This is the reason, for example, for the recent increased reports of pregnancy discrimination brought against UK, US and Australian organisations (Brough, Kinman, McDowall & Chan, 2021).

Industrial relations legislation

Some industrial relations laws legislate against an individual repeatedly behaving unreasonably towards a worker. Reasonable behaviour for a manager may include the allocation of work or the process of providing feedback to workers, if it is carried out in a manner that does not leave the individual feeling victimised or humiliated. A manager's unreasonable behaviour must have created a *risk* to health and safety. It is not necessary to have already had an effect on the worker's health and safety. This allows for an organisation to take proactive action by which abuse can be prevented before it causes serious harm (Catanzariti & Egan, 2015). Taking an industrial relations approach to cases of clear gross misconduct (e.g., sustained extreme cases of workplace bullying by a manager) can be effective, through a process of investigation, warning, discipline, sanction and/or dismissal. However, a formal investigation causes immense stress to all parties: the accused, the complainant and employees interviewed as part of the investigation process. This is especially problematic when the behaviour complained about has happened behind closed doors, without witnesses, or is the subject of hearsay. Whether the complaint is upheld or not, it is often extremely difficult for those engaging with this legal process to continue to work together, either at the time of the investigation or, if the complaint is not upheld, afterwards.

CONCLUSION

There is now a significant body of research describing the conceptual explanations for destructive leadership. This chapter has reviewed the definitions of destructive leadership, descriptions of common destructive leadership behaviours and the consequences of those behaviours for leaders and for their targets. The role of followers in the enactment of destructive leadership behaviours has also been assessed and consideration has been given to the organisational contexts and organisational responses to this wicked problem. However, there has been less focus on the antecedents that predispose leaders to engage in destructive leadership behaviours, and these antecedents are discussed in the next chapter (Chapter 3).

3

ANTECEDENTS TO DESTRUCTIVE LEADERSHIP

CHAPTER OVERVIEW

Researchers investigating a leader trait approach to leadership have suggested that dark side personality traits (socially undesirable traits that can have negative implications for work success and the wellbeing of employees) exhibit curvilinear relationships with key outcomes (e.g., leader and follower performance, follower engagement and followers' wellbeing). That is, there are negative consequences for both extremely low and extremely high 'bright side' personality traits (behavioural traits leaders exhibit when they are performing at their best) and positive consequences for moderate 'dark side' traits. The key personality traits, characteristics and motives that predict or inhibit a predisposition to exhibit destructive leadership behaviours are discussed in this chapter, including possible self-regulation processes as mediators, based on trait activation theory. It is important to understand the mechanisms by which leaders may activate derailing traits and engage in destructive leadership behaviours through overusing their strengths or failure of self-regulation.

ANTECEDENTS TO DESTRUCTIVE LEADERSHIP

The purpose of this chapter is to discuss the antecedents for leaders engaging in destructive behaviours, including the bright and dark side personality traits as antecedents of destructive leadership, the process of leader derailment and personality traits that may prevent or inhibit engagement in destructive leadership behaviours. This chapter discusses two specific questions: (1) what are the antecedent traits, characteristics and motives that may predispose an individual leader to engage in destructive leadership behaviours? (2) What traits or regulatory processes may inhibit the predisposition of leaders to employ harmful behaviours?

It is clear that many variables contribute to the motivation to act – namely, aroused motive for action (need for achievement, affiliation and power), probability of success (e.g., skills), incentive value (e.g., rewards) and other variables (e.g., environmental opportunities). Different events or situations may trigger different responses from a particular leader, with variable outcomes. Of particular interest is what stimulates leaders to follow, or not follow, their dispositional tendencies. It has been proposed, for example, that destructive leadership behaviours are often employed by leaders to resolve goal blockages that thwart their own achievement aspirations. To better understand the individual traits, characteristics and motivations that contribute to leaders exhibiting destructive leadership, it is useful to consider psychological and psycho-sociological theoretical perspectives.

ANTECEDENT TRAITS AND MOTIVES TO DESTRUCTIVE LEADERSHIP

The areas of psychology that focus on personality traits, characteristics, preferences, motivations and behaviours have explained many features of destructive leadership. Theoretical explanations of the dark side of leadership have described the common negative personality characteristics exhibited by destructive leaders (Judge, Piccolo & Kosalka, 2009). Maladaptive individual differences have also been conceptualised as extreme variants of adaptive or bright side traits. The bright side of leadership has been defined as the ability to build and maintain a high-performing team, using personality characteristics based on the Big Five model of personality: higher levels of extraversion, agreeableness, conscientiousness and openness and lower levels of neuroticism, with an absence of dark side traits (Costa & McCrae, 1992; Hogan, Curphy & Hogan, 1994). When compared with the Big Five, dark side traits tend to be correlated with low levels of agreeableness, conscientiousness and openness (Judge & LePine, 2007; Judge et al., 2009). It is only when bright and dark side trait characteristics become extreme, or when certain behaviours are used excessively, that they create problems. Examples discussed in the literature include the dark side of leadership (Hogan, Kaiser, Sherman & Harms, 2021), the dark side of charisma (Fragouli, 2018; Hogan et al., 2021; Pundt, 2014), the dark side of transformational leadership (de Villiers, 2014; Khoo & Burch, 2008; Lin, Scott & Matta, 2019; Tourish, 2013) and the dark side of authentic leadership (Ford & Harding, 2011; Nyberg & Sveningsson, 2014).

A curvilinear relationship between leadership trait characteristics and performance/leadership effectiveness has been proposed (Benson & Campbell, 2007). Leadership traits and behaviours that may be crucial to success in one situation may be unrelated or even negatively related to success in other contexts – that is, *the dark side of bright characteristics* and *the bright side of dark characteristics* (e.g., Benson & Campbell, 2007; Furnham, Trickey & Hyde, 2012; Kaiser, LeBreton & Hogan, 2015). More specifically, it has been suggested that a leader's personality traits exhibit a curvilinear relationship with their followers' levels of engagement, wellbeing and performance. That is, there are negative consequences for *both* low levels and high levels of bright side personality traits and positive consequences for moderate levels of dark side personality traits (e.g., Judge et al., 2009; Hogan & Hogan, 2001). For example, high levels of assertiveness, a person's tendency to pursue and speak out for their own interests, may bring short-term goal achievement but can also have an adverse effect on relationships over time (Ames & Flynn, 2007).

Trait activation theory proposes that trait-relevant cues in a particular situation lead to an individual expressing a trait and, depending on the effectiveness and appropriateness of the trait expressed, determine the effectiveness of the resulting behaviour. Van Knippenberg (2012, p. 688) proposed trait expression was a function of:

> the personality trait x situation trait relevance (trait relevant cues) x situation strength (the extent to which the situation is clear on what is appropriate and inappropriate behaviour).

This model is equally applicable to the activation of dark side personality traits when expressing destructive leadership behaviours (see Figure 3.1).

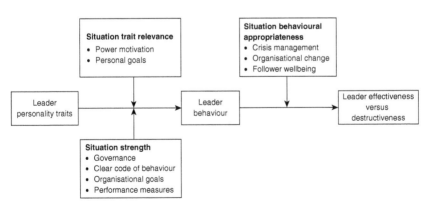

Figure 3.1   Trait activation model of destructive leadership.

Source: Adapted from van Knippenberg (2012).

Leader independence

A leader's desire for independence has typically been described as one of the bright side personality traits, particularly in Western society, where hierarchical power with a focus on individual achievement is rewarded (Fletcher & Kaufer, 2003). The trait of *independence* can be defined as a desire for autonomy and decision-making, without input from others (Schmit, Kihm & Robie, 2000). Independence has been incorporated under the Big Five factors as being related to openness to experience (Schmit et al., 2000) and emotional stability (Hogan et al., 1994), and is commonly associated with effective leadership performance (e.g., Judge, Bono, Illies & Gerhadt, 2002).

It is paradoxical that as leaders emerge based on their independence and personal achievements, they are promoted into positions that require them to be interdependent, to influence and work with others, so that in order to be effective, they can no longer rely solely on their own skills and efforts (Fletcher & Kaufer, 2002). There is also an established link between personality traits and motivation – that is, individuals high in independence are likely to be motivated by personalised power and the need for achievement of personal goals (McClelland & Boyatzis, 1982), as compared to individuals high in interdependence, who are more likely to be movitated by socialised power and achieve their goals through others (McClelland, 1970). Leaders with a strong need for independence are likely to ignore competing points of view and become irritated or argumentative if others persist with these views (Hogan & Hogan, 2001). If the leader remains wedded to their own agenda and fails to listen to others, they become susceptible to derailment (Hogan et al., 1994). Thus, leaders with very high levels of independence may be predisposed to exhibit destructive behaviours because they are more likely to be motivated to use any means at their disposal to achieve their personal goals, and to prioritise their personal goals over the needs of the group (Hogan et al., 1994; Krasikova, Green & LeBreton, 2013). Figure 3.2 displays a theoretical model describing trait and motive antecedents for leader engagement in destructive leadership behaviours.

Leader need for achievement

A leader's need for achievement is another trait that is described as one of the bright side personality traits for leadership (House & Howell, 1992). The need for achievement is the tendency to have a strong drive to realise personally meaningful goals, be challenged by difficult goals, be energised by accomplishing goals, take satisfaction from doing something difficult, push outside of

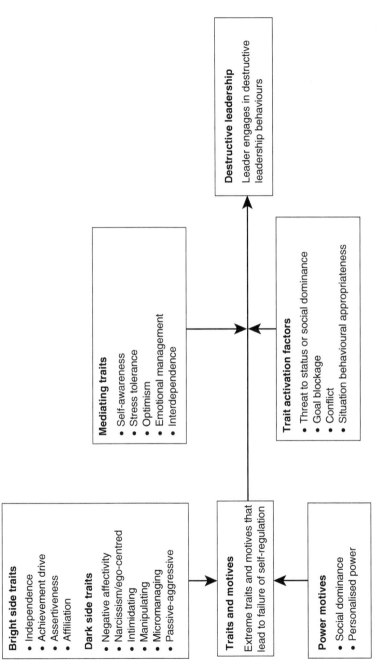

Figure 3.2 Theoretical model for trait and power antecedents for engaging in destructive leadership behaviours.

one's comfort zone to achieve a goal and develop better ways of doing things to attain standards of excellence (Schmit et al., 2000). The dark side of the need for achievement is the tendency to ignore interpersonal relationships and ignore interpersonal and/or political issues in the name of task completion (McClelland, 1992). An extreme need for achievement encourages managers to prioritise the accomplishment of goals through their own personal efforts, rather than through the efforts of others, to exploit, coerce and command others with their determination and relentless focus on tasks and goals and to be oblivious to the concerns of others (Furtner, Rauthmann & Sachse, 2011; McClelland, 1992; Spreier, Fontaine & Malloy, 2006).

Leader need for affiliation

An important motivation for engaging in constructive leadership behaviours that lead to engaged, energised and cohesive teams is the desire to build relationships. Therefore, affiliation is viewed as a bright side trait for managers. Leaders with a need for affiliation are regarded as having a non-conscious motive for establishing, maintaining and restoring close relationships with others. Two of the Big Five dimensions, extraversion and agreeableness, are strongly related to interpersonal behaviour. Extraversion (enthusiasm) and agreeableness (compassion) are related to trait affiliation (DeYoung, Weisberg, Quilty & Peterson, 2013; Judge & Bono, 2000; Trapnell & Wiggins, 1990). However, an extreme need for affiliation may compromise a leader's ability to make objective decisions about others – that is, it may lead to favouritism (McClelland, 1992). The need for affiliation may also lead to the tendency to avoid conflict and to engage in passive-aggressive behaviours such as avoiding confrontations, conveying acceptance or co-operation by lack of objection, expressing support for others' ideas and behaving in a contradictory manner or appearing to behave in unco-operative and self-serving ways (Schmit et al., 2000). In addition, a fear of confrontation may lead managers to adopt a laissez-faire style of leadership, including delaying or failing to give important constructive feedback, or failing to support an employee in a difficult interaction (Skogstad, Einarsen, Torsheim, Aasland & Hetland, 2007).

Leader power motives

The endowment of power on leaders to achieve organisational goals can cause some leaders to feel tension between wanting to achieve group success and wanting to maintain their own power and status (Maner & Mead, 2010). Individual differences commonly associated with power motives are the desire for social dominance and prestige (Hu & Liu, 2017; Maner & Mead, 2010).

Leaders seeking social dominance commonly achieve power by the use of force and the manipulation of resources to benefit themselves. Leaders concerned with prestige, in contrast, influence through garnering respect and using their knowledge and expertise to benefit others and help the group achieve its goals. The distinction between the desire for dominance and prestige is similar to the distinction made between personalised power (using power for personal gain) and socialised power (using power to benefit other people).

Social dominance orientation

Leaders with a high social dominance orientation believe that employees should obey authority figures' directions without question, and therefore believe that their exhibition of dominance over others is an appropriate method to gain their employees' obedience. Such individuals are especially motivated to enhance their status, in order to maintain their superiority in the hierarchy. Hu and Liu (2017) proposed that a leader's desire for enhancing their status mediates the relationship between a leader's social dominance orientation and their abusive behaviour. Status can be enhanced by either exerting dominance over others (use of force or intimidation) or gaining prestige. This mediation between social dominance and abusive behaviour is stronger under two conditions: first, when the leader is experiencing positional instability (e.g., working in a competitive organisational environment where their performance is continuously monitored and where they will be replaced if they produce unsatisfactory performance) and, second, when they perceive they do not have status or internal respect in the eyes of others within the organisation. Leaders with a high need for social dominance and status who perceive they have low internal respect from others may feel that their position is under threat and that others have negative intentions against them. As a result, they are more likely to engage in abusive behaviours (e.g., maximising power at the expense of ethical considerations, engaging in aggressive and intimidatory tactics). When a leader's position is unstable and their power could be threatened, leaders with high social dominance motivation have a tendency to exclude rivals, such as top performers, and take on the role of directing tasks as a way of protecting their own power. However, when there is intergroup competition, the presence of a rival outgroup shifts the leader's mindset from viewing their group members as competitors to seeing them as allies (Maner & Mead, 2010).

Personalised power motive

Leaders driven by personalised power draw strength from controlling others and making them feel weak (McClelland, 1970). A personalised power orientation is related to aversive leadership (Bligh, Kohles, Pearce, Justin & Stovall,

2007). Medina, Lopez and Medina (2020) provided examples of power methods that leaders rely on when using their power in unethical ways (personalised power) by engaging in abusive behaviours. *Power methods* refer to the ways managers feel entitled to behave when exercising their power over subordinate employees. Medina et al. described 10 power methods: controlling every task, activity and interaction the employee engages in (micromanagement); taking responsibility away from the employee; denying their requests; discriminating against the employee by engaging in abusive behaviour or excluding them from meetings; ignoring the results of tasks completed at their request; inconsistent behaviour (e.g., mood swings) and communication patterns; overuse of negative feedback, in contrast to positive feedback from others; reducing the employee by implying the subordinate has less competence or a lower position than they really have; utilising employees' dependence on the manager by extorting personal favours; exploiting their position and power by commanding the employee; and using their internal political influence. Only when power is moderated by inhibition of impulsive actions is power used responsibly (socialised power).

Patterns of motivation

McClelland and Boyatzis (1982) proposed a motive pattern called the *leadership motive pattern*. This model describes how leaders were more likely to be promoted to higher management levels and achieve successful performance if they were high in power, low in affiliation and high in activity inhibition (the ability to moderate multiple motives). Leadership styles emerge from the interaction of the need for individual achievement, affiliation, personalised power and socialised power (Spreier et al., 2006). For example, an extremely strong drive to achieve, to improve personal performance and to exceed standards of excellence may cause leaders to micromanage, to pace themselves and others and to focus on goals and outcomes rather than people. A strong need for affiliation may motivate leaders to maintain close, friendly relationships, but in the extreme it could lead to passive behaviours, such as avoiding confrontation or avoiding giving negative feedback. However, more recently, researchers have proposed that a medium to high need for affiliation is crucial to leadership (Spangler, Tikhomirov, Sotak & Palrecha, 2014; Steinmann, Kleinert & Maier, 2020). Thus, a focus on initiating and maintaining relationships is important when leaders are required to empower teams, show consideration for workforce diversity and foster employee commitment in uncertain work environments, especially those associated with economic and societal upheavals (e.g., digitalisation, pandemics and natural disasters). Leaders motivated by socialised power and affiliation are perceived to engage in effective leadership behaviours, compared to those striving for personal accomplishments (Steinmann et al., 2020). However, an uninhibited motive for status and self-aggrandisement (personalised power), uninhibited affiliation or uninhibited achievement drive may lead to engagement in destructive behaviours (Spangler et al., 2014).

Negative affectivity trait

Negative affectivity – the tendency of an individual to differentially dwell on the negative aspects of themselves and their life, to experience negative emotions such as anxiety, fear and anger and to react impulsively to such emotions – is also directly associated with destructive leadership performance (Schyns & Schilling, 2013; Tepper, 2007; Watson & Clark, 1984). Individuals with high levels of the trait negative affectivity are particularly sensitive to the minor failures and frustrations of daily life, are typically viewed as more independent, are more likely to perceive failure as a stressor and in stress situations tend to exhibit a decreased need for affiliation (Watson & Clark, 1984). Krasikova et al. (2013) proposed that negative affectivity (e.g., anxiety and worry) is an important antecedent to a range of destructive leadership behaviours. If a leader perceives the progress from their current state towards their desired goal as being too slow, levels of negative affectivity increase, stimulating actions to reduce this goal-attainment discrepancy. In this context, increased negative affectivity is associated with either the anticipation of impending adversities or the anticipation of an inability to attract rewards, resulting in an increased predisposition to engage in destructive behaviours. For example, leaders may develop sensitivities due to a set of unconscious emotionally charged beliefs and expectations, generalised from their past experience, that protect them from repeating a painful experience. Such leaders are more likely to interpret environmental cues negatively when fatigued or stressed, and to react intensely and compulsively as a form of self-protection. Negative affectivity is commonly portrayed as a trait that reduces an individual's ability to self-regulate or inhibit their behaviours and reactions. Therefore, it has been suggested that self-regulation is a crucial element for both the prediction of leader derailment and the management of destructive leadership behaviours (Krasikova et al., 2013).

THE ROLE OF LEADER SELF-REGULATION

In general, self-regulation refers to the process by which individuals initiate, adjust, terminate or otherwise alter actions to promote their attainment of personal goals (Collins & Jackson, 2015; Heatherton & Baumeister, 1996). Multiple explanations for how self-regulation is enacted have been proposed by research-ers, incorporating personal characteristics (e.g., self-efficacy, self-esteem and self-awareness; Karoly, 1993), skills (e.g., political skill; Whitman, Halbesleben & Shanine, 2013) and behaviours (e.g., self-talk, self-observation, self-monitoring, self-recording; Karoly, 1993; Rogelberg et al., 2013; Zimmerman, 2000). Individual differences in goal-directed behaviour may depend on an individual's *regulatory focus*: self-regulation with a promotion focus to realise positive outcomes (e.g., accomplishment of aspirations), compared to self-regulation with a prevention focus in order to avoid negative outcomes (e.g., threat to wellbeing or loss of reputation; Higgins, 1987, 1997; van Knippenberg, 2012).

The role of intrapersonal self-regulatory processes in controlling impulsivity has been identified as an important characteristic in achieving personal goals (Bandura, 1991; Karoly, 1993). It is argued that the capacity to engage in intra-personal self-regulatory mechanisms (e.g., direct purposeful actions from within to override, alter or inhibit dysfunctional responses or behaviours) enables bet-ter goal selection, goal co-ordination and goal achievement (Bandura, 1991; Heatherton & Baumeister, 1996; Karoly, 1993). However, it is also clear that goals can have *negative* consequences. Goal difficulty and the extent to which rewards are contingent upon goal attainment contribute to destructive leader-ship behaviours through their impact on levels of stress. For example, increased negative affectivity is associated with the anticipation of impending adversities or the anticipation of an inability to attract rewards due to failure to perform through goal achievement (Bardes & Piccolo, 2010). Perceived goal block-age is a common antecedent of destructive leadership, especially in leaders with a high need for individual achievement, such as those motivated by per-sonalised power, or leaders with low self-esteem who rely primarily on their individual achievements to boost their self-worth (Crocker, 2002; Krasikova el al., 2013). Leaders with high negative affectivity have a negativity bias when interpreting events and are more likely to perceive their goals as being blocked by the organisation or their followers. Leaders with high negative affectivity and self-regulation impairment are more likely to react to goal blockage by choosing to engage in destructive leadership behaviours. Similarly, a failure of self-regulatory processes may also result from a depletion of resources to deal with work-related stressors – that is, role overload, organisational constraints or interpersonal conflict (Baumeister, Muraven & Tice, 2000; Byrne et al., 2014; Collins & Jackson, 2015; Wang, Sinclair & Deese, 2010).

In addition to intrapersonal self-regulation mechanisms, self-regulation has also been defined as a social or interpersonal process (Tsui & Ashford, 1994; Wang et al., 2010). Given these propositions, the ability to engage self-regulatory processes through activating self-regulatory traits and behaviours is likely to mediate the relationship between a strong need for power and personal goal achievement and the predisposition to use constructive or destructive leadership behaviours when facing frustration or perceived failure. The difference between effective leaders, who use their dark side tendencies as strengths in specific situations, and derailed leaders may partly reside in the leader's ability to develop self-insight (e.g., awareness of their own conscious and unconscious motivations), which can set in motion a process of corrective change. Effectiveness is also likely to reside in a leader's ability to regulate their impulsive behaviour and need for personal power, even in competitive or stressful situations, so that a leader's strengths are utilised only in appropriate contexts and goals are achieved in a way that does not cause harm (Judge et al., 2009; McClelland, 1970, 1975, 1985; Spreier et al., 2006).

Self-regulatory processes, such as emotional control (also referred to as emotion management or emotion regulation; Lawrence, Troth, Jordan & Collins, 2011), can also impact functional or dysfunctional outcomes, depending on an individual's ability to regulate negative emotions in response to organisational stressors (Jordan & Lindebaum, 2015; Ruderman, Hammum, Leslie & Steed, 2001). For example, low levels of stress tolerance (i.e., the inability to tolerate stressful situations without undue physical or emotional reactions) and low levels of self-awareness (i.e., the inability to read one's emotions and motivations and understand their effects on others) have both been associated with self-regulation impairment (Wang et al., 2010).

In addition, leaders low in self-awareness are unlikely to be aware of their limitations, which may lead them to take on unachievable goals or prevent them delivering the outcomes they desire. They are also more likely to interpret constructive feedback as a threat or a sign of failure and become angry or dismissive, resorting to destructive behaviours (Ruderman et al., 2001). In a test of this specific association, Harms, Spain and Hannah (2011) demonstrated that self-awareness training was effective in mitigating the negative effects of destructive personality traits within a sample of military cadets. Alternatively, resilient, emotionally stable leaders are less likely to experience intense negative emotions to stressors. Therefore, personal characteristics such as optimism, emotional control and stress tolerance are likely to predict an improved ability to engage in self-regulation processes when under stress (Collins & Jackson, 2015; Kaiser et al., 2015; King & Rothstein, 2010; Wang et al., 2010).

IMPLICATIONS FOR PRACTICE

Creating an environment where negative affectivity is likely to be triggered in leaders (e.g., when their goals are thwarted) increases the likelihood of activation of dark side traits, leading to engagement in derailing behaviours through inhibited self-regulation. Organisations may unintentionally foster destructive behaviours by focusing on the achievement of strategic and operational goals at any cost, by only measuring outcomes and/or by punishing failures and non-achievement of key performance indicators. Setting difficult goals or placing pressure on managers to achieve their individual goals may lead to engagement in dispositional negative affectivity, if failure or underperformance is likely to result in punitive measures and/or non-achievement of an incentive, such as a financial bonus (Bardes & Piccolo, 2010; Krasikova et al., 2013; Mawritz, Folger & Lathan, 2014). Organisations that place equal emphasis on how organisational goals are achieved – that is, the behaviours demonstrated in goal achievement, together with goal outcomes – are less likely to encourage destructive behaviours to ensure goal attainment.

A key practice for preventing destructive leadership is providing organisations with strategies to screen out manager candidates likely to engage in destructive leadership behaviours (Judge & LePine, 2007). For example, it is prudent to screen out candidates with extreme levels of bright side traits (e.g., independence, desire for achievement), high levels of dark side traits (e.g., negative affectivity, ego-centred behaviour, intimidation, manipulation, micromanagement and passive-aggression; Schmit et al., 2000) and low levels of self-management traits (e.g., self-awareness, emotional control, optimism, stress tolerance). Assessment tools for this screening are discussed in more detail in Chapter 9. Should an organisation decide to hire or promote a candidate with extreme derailing personality traits, perhaps due to the individual's rare technical expertise and skills, additional support and professional development strategies may be required during their onboarding process, such as providing coaching by a psychologist, to prevent engagement in destructive leadership behaviours.

To develop leadership styles that enhance employee wellbeing, it is recommended that practitioners include training in their leadership development programmes on both constructive leadership behaviour (such as transformational and transactional leadership styles) *and* destructive leadership behaviour. Leader development programmes should include mechanisms to increase managers' self-awareness of their blind spots, the impact of their leadership style and their capacity for self-regulation to effectively self-manage their behaviour and include activities designed to protect leaders from derailing (e.g., leadership style profiles, resiliency training, reflective practice, self-regulatory mechanisms; Kaiser et al., 2015). We discuss organisational leadership interventions in depth in Section 2 of this book.

CONCLUSION

Organisations and employees suffer when leaders engage in destructive leadership, overusing their strengths or abusing their power. This chapter has reviewed the current understanding of a leader's motives to engage in destructive leadership behaviours – for example, intrapersonal traits and characteristics, power motives and situational factors associated with failure of self-regulation. Researchers and practitioners can build on the research literature to design empirical investigations to test hypothesised antecedents to destructive leadership and to inform interventions that may minimise leader engagement in destructive leadership behaviours. One effective way to guard against incidents of destructive leadership behaviours is to screen out candidates with dark side tendencies when selecting and promoting managers. This is important, given the dire consequences of destructive leadership on the leaders themselves, their targets and their organisation.

4

THE IMPACT OF DESTRUCTIVE LEADERSHIP

CHAPTER OVERVIEW

It is clearly evident that destructive leadership has negative impacts on the wellbeing and performance of targeted employees, destroys employee commitment to their organisation and reduces the effectiveness of teams. Destructive leadership leads to a toxic organisational culture that can spiral organisations into an ever decreasing ability to meet the challenges of their business environment and achieve their organisational objectives. In this chapter, we discuss the impacts of destructive leadership for a leader's targets, colleagues, families and communities, as well as the impacts for their organisation's culture, performance and financial commitments.

THE IMPACT OF DESTRUCTIVE LEADERSHIP

Up to 70% of employees report that their manager is the worst aspect of their job, and abusive treatment by supervisors is one of the most commonly cited causes of stress and compensation claims (Einarsen, Skogstad & Aasland, 2010; Webster, Brough & Daly, 2016). It is also estimated that up to 70% of all leaders exhibit derailing behaviours, through alienating others and losing the loyalty and commitment of their followers (Trickey & Hyde, 2009). One study found that up to 25% of their manager sample exhibited at least one dark side personality trait (De Fruyt, Wille & Furnham, 2013). Similarly, Aasland, Skogstad, Notelaers, Nielsen and Einarsen (2010) reported that 60% of a sample of Norwegian employees indicated that their immediate supervisor had exhibited some form of consistent destructive behaviour during the preceding six months. If these reported prevalence estimates are accurate, it implies that many managers engage in some form of destructive leadership during their career that may cause harm to their own and others' wellbeing. Leadership development programmes have flourished in the last few years, promoting constructive leadership behaviours. These include specific programmes focused on transformational, transactional and/or authentic leadership styles, which emphasise that a leader must consider the needs of their followers, and engage in ethical, values- and character-based leadership (Avolio, Walumbwa & Weber, 2009; Caza & Jackson, 2011; Hannah & Avolio, 2010; Quick & Wright, 2011). Despite these programmes, destructive leadership experiences remain prevalent in organisations, with negative outcomes for individual workers, teams, organisations and ultimately the community.

IMPACT ON TARGETS

Individual differences can affect employees' perceptions and their reactions to destructive leadership behaviours. Employees who accommodate a destructive leader, or are unaware of the destructive goals of the leader, often receive rewards from the leader. Alternatively, employees who resist destructive leaders' directions or express their dissent with leaders' destructive goals are at risk of repercussions, including losing their jobs. Reported harmful consequences for individual targets subjected to destructive leader behaviours over time commonly include psychological distress (e.g., reduced self-esteem, self-doubt, stress, anxiety, depression, difficulty concentrating, self-regulation impairment), emotional harm (e.g., rumination, mistrust, anger, fear, shame), physical health problems (e.g., chronic fatigue and low energy, colds, gastric upsets, hair loss, headaches, insomnia, skin rashes and self-medicating behaviour) and negative work performance (e.g., reduced effectiveness, disengagement, burnout, reduced job, work and life satisfaction, work and family conflict and reduced discretionary effort (Krasikova, Green & LeBreton, 2013; Martinko, Harvey, Brees & Mackey, 2013; Schyns & Schilling, 2013; Tepper, Simon & Park, 2017; Webster et al., 2016).

Definitions of destructive leadership include the criteria that the destructive behaviours must be systematic, repeated and sustained – for example, over a period of months or years. However, extremely abusive behaviours, such as yelling at and berating a subordinate in public, may create an immediate acute stress response. Exposure to even one chronic stressor that is perceived by the individual as threatening can be damaging to wellbeing. However, employees are often subjected to multiple psychosocial stressors when experiencing destructive leader behaviours. Abusive leader behaviours (e.g., humiliating, threatening or intimidating behaviours) are not the only form of destructive leadership. Exploitative leadership (e.g., leadership with the primary intention to further the leader's self-interest) can also produce negative emotions and turnover intentions in followers (Schmid, Pircher Verdorfer & Peus, 2018). Laissez-faire leadership, a passive, indirect form of destructive leadership, has been found to be associated with role ambiguity or conflict, interpersonal conflict between co-workers and a higher incidence of bullying in the workplace (Hawkes & Spedding, in press; Skogstad, Einarsen, Torsheim, Aasland & Hetland, 2007).

Leaders with narcissistic tendencies have a negative impact on their employees by failing to maintain effective working relationships. Due to their desire to lead, their need for power, their bold decisions and their confident, assertive and sometimes charismatic demeanour, leaders with a narcissistic style may be rated by employees as good leaders initially. Over time and with more interaction, peer and staff ratings become more negative, despite the leader's self-ratings remaining higher than others' ratings. Narcissistic leaders constantly crave adoration and anyone who contradicts their self-image or sense of superiority will initiate an obsessional response to real or imagined slights or criticism. Dissenters are typically targeted with attacks from the leader, in an attempt to reassert their dominance. Employees feel manipulated and exploited, leading to feelings of self-doubt, fear and anxiety. Subordinates are often reluctant to speak up, question the leader or offer feedback due to a fear of retribution (McFarlin & Sweeney, 2010).

The impact of leaders with a manipulative or psychopathic style of leadership is even more destructive. Leaders displaying psychopathic characteristics (e.g., lying, manipulative and unethical behaviours, seeking personal power and control) result in a disengaged, disheartened and disillusioned workforce, characterised by employees with higher levels of fear, distress, despair, insecurity, frustration, anger and low wellbeing. Employees who are perceived by an organisational psychopath as a threat to the progression of the leader's career are likely to be targeted, threatened, undermined and eventually removed from the organisation (Boddy, 2015; Boddy, Miles, Sanyal & Hartog, 2015).

Impact on families

The adverse impacts experienced by the individual targets of destructive leader behaviours do not only occur within the work domain. In addition to the spread of negativity among employees at work, negative emotions are also taken home, where they negatively impact upon family members. This spillover of chronic work stress can produce negative interpersonal relationships at home, which in turn may contribute to a downward spiral of stress, anxiety and depression occurring in both the work and home spheres (see the crossover or stress contagion literature; Brough, Muller & Westman, 2018). Targets of destructive leadership often find that their difficult work situation consumes all of their thoughts and private time. Partners can feel frustrated that they can't assist in solving the issue, especially when targets are unable to communicate details of the specific work abuse they are experiencing (Carlson, Ferguson, Hunter & Whitten, 2012).

An additional consequence of the psychological distress experienced by a target is a displacement of their frustration and stress on to family members. That is, they may unconsciously redirect their reactions away from the source of their stress (i.e., their manager) on to an alternative, less powerful target (i.e., their spouse or children). In other words, they avoid showing aggression directly towards their manager for fear of retaliation, disciplinary action or losing their job, so instead undermine their family members via exhibiting anger, criticism or the silent treatment. Thus, the experience of destructive leadership can negatively impact an employee's family relationships and family activities (Hoobler & Brass, 2006; Restubog, Scott & Zagenczyk, 2011).

If an individual target cannot remain at work and takes stress leave or resigns from the organisation, there may also be a significant financial cost for the family to endure. Further research is required to assess these and other details of the impact of destructive leadership on families, such as the effects of emotional contagion from the target to family members, the repercussions from incidents of substance abuse (i.e., problem drinking, self-medication), the effects of a depressed individual on family members and the impact of financial strain on the family system.

Consequences for the community

Despite highly funded and well publicised efforts to address physical diseases, such as COVID-19, cancer, diabetes and heart disease, significantly less effort is put into understanding and addressing the psychological disease of destructive leadership. Yet, as has been discussed above, the effects of destructive leadership can be equally harmful to the health and wellbeing of individuals and, through flow-on effects, to their families and the wider community. There is a significant societal cost for employees who are unable to work for a prolonged period of time – for example, as a result of workplace stress (mental health) claims. Indirect costs associated with destructive leadership include medical costs, premature retirement and a greater need for social services and welfare. For broader society, there is also the cost of a lack of business ethics and corporate responsibility experienced by customers, suppliers, stakeholders and the community at large (Burgess, Brough, Biggs & Hawkes, 2020; Kellerman, 2004).

IMPACT ON DESTRUCTIVE LEADERS

Destructive leadership also impacts negatively on the offending leader themselves, including reported low satisfaction with the leader and subordinate resistance to the leader's attempts at influencing their work behaviours. Moreover, the negative perceptions an individual develops of their leader can spread to the team through social and emotional contagion processes, creating a shared negative perception of the leader (Schmid, Pircher Verdorfer & Peus, 2019). As a result, subordinates and colleagues may engage in direct aggression, resistance or retaliatory acts towards the perpetrator, including explicit counterproductive work behaviours. While direct resistance towards the leader may incur a risk of punishment by the leader, clandestine counterproductive work behaviour is often a safer way to demonstrate retaliation. However, if the employee intends to leave the organisation, they are likely to be less fearful of the abusive manager and more likely to retaliate against them, by, for example, gossiping about them or refusing to interact with them (Lian et al., 2014; Restubog et al., 2011). Aggression directed towards a manager may be mediated by the level of hostility they feel towards their manager and their capacity to control this hostility. High levels of employee conscientiousness, agreeableness and self-regulatory capability may mitigate the experience of abuse by their manager and the target's motivation to retaliate.

If the leader continues to engage in abusive or exploitative behaviour, relationships are damaged at all levels of the organisation and the leader's own career can derail (Erickson, Shaw, Murray & Branch, 2015; Schyns & Schilling, 2013; Tepper, Moss, Lockhart & Carr, 2007). A more serious consequence arises when leaders driven by self-interest and a personal agenda gain higher levels of power and status. They are more likely to engage in ethical lapses and indiscretions, which can include accounting fraud, embezzlement, tax evasion, over-billing, substance abuse, sexual impropriety or perjury. Such behaviours occur when the leader perceives a low risk of being caught and few consequences, which can lead to their downfall (Daniel, 2017).

IMPACT ON TEAMS

Under the leadership of destructive leaders, inter-team and intra-team conflict often escalates, increasing employee stress, reducing social support from colleagues and negatively impacting on team performance and goal achievements. The work outcomes of a team are not just influenced by the direct interaction of individuals with the leader; leadership behaviour directed towards other team members also influences employees' attitudes and emotions. Targets of abuse may wish to express their anger and frustration by retaliating against the abuser. However, because of the power differential occurring between them and their manager, they may choose instead to act out their aggression on other team members. Being exposed to high levels of team abuse can cause members to learn devaluing behaviours and to treat fellow team members with aggression and hostility. When interactions between team members are characterised by interpersonal attacks, the team experiences high levels of conflict within their interpersonal relationships. The laissez-faire style of leadership is especially identified as a precursor to workplace bullying in teams. The manager's lack of intervention allows workplace stressors to emerge, contributing to a climate of high levels of interpersonal conflict. When the manager does not sanction abusive behaviour by members of the team and, importantly, does not proactively manage this conflict, interpersonal conflicts escalate and team members can perceive themselves as being bullied by their co-workers (Einarsen et al., 2010; Farh & Chen, 2014; Skogstad et al., 2007).

Exploitative leaders, driven by self-interest, may continuously delegate tedious tasks that they do not want to do themselves, or they may hinder subordinates' career advancement by, for example, keeping a team member that is useful to them in their team. They may also claim the team's work as their own, reducing the job satisfaction of team members due to the injustice of the manager's actions (Schmid et al., 2019). When increasing amounts of time are spent on team members venting and discussing the latest 'bad behaviour', work productivity is reduced. Team members protect themselves from their leaders' destructive behaviours by withdrawing from their work, increasingly staying away from the workplace or ultimately leaving the organisation.

Leaders with narcissistic tendencies are not team players. Narcissistic leaders are willing to step over others to get what they want, are oblivious to others' perspectives or views and fail to acknowledge the contributions of others. They are also comfortable engaging in questionable conduct in order to achieve their goals and to engage in counterproductive work behaviours. Therefore, they tend to create in-groups (who they see as fostering achievement of their objectives) and out-groups (who they see as opposing them), creating divisions and conflict in teams. Leaders with manipulative and psychopathic tendencies are capable of irreparably damaging the morale and emotional wellbeing of their work teams through their extremely abusive behaviours (Boddy, 2015).

CONSEQUENCES FOR ORGANISATIONS

Destructive leadership creates many issues for organisations. As destructive leaders focus on accomplishing self-serving, individual goals – in contrast to goals that enhance the overall, long-term profitability and sustainability of the organisation – the organisation suffers. Creativity is quashed when employees become more risk averse due to their fear of making mistakes; thus, an avoidance of risk-taking is preferable to punishment. Destructive leadership creates an environment of fear, decreased work cohesion and a decline in employee performance and wellbeing. Employee performance diminishes for those who spend their time job hunting and/or being absent from work. High turnover rates are accompanied with the costs of recruitment and training new employees. In turn, the presence of destructive leaders can negatively affect an organisation's ability to attract and recruit high potential candidates or to develop the performance potential of employees once hired (Erickson et al., 2015).

Impact on culture

One of the most significant impacts of destructive leadership is the toxic organisational culture that is often produced. This culture in turn enhances the likelihood of more destructive leaders emerging and being recruited. Toxic cultures are often characterised by increased political behaviour, where cronyism and nepotism become the norm (Akuffo & Kivipõld, 2017). Employees often feel disrespect for those who have hired a destructive leader, impacting negatively on their view of their organisation. Employees' organisational commitment reduces as they perceive the organisation does not intervene to protect employees. Research indicates that the work ethic and culture of an organisation can change very rapidly, within weeks or months of a candidate with psychopathic tendencies being appointed to a leadership position (Boddy, 2015; Erickson et al., 2015; Schyns & Schilling, 2013).

When destructive leaders hold power in an organisation, there is often a disconnect between what the organisation claims to want from its leaders and the types of behaviour it actually rewards. While intensely results-oriented managers are not easy to work for, they can be perceived by their boss and employees as professional because their focus is on achieving results for the organisation. On the other hand, leaders who are more concerned with advancing their own personal agenda will create a culture of competition, where results are to be achieved at any cost. Leaders who focus on results may promote the need to do whatever is necessary to get the job done, turning a blind eye to how the results are obtained. Bad behaviour is inadvertently encouraged by the manager's relentless focus on excellence, internal competition and results at any cost, together with a perception that there are no consequences for the use of aggressive or intimidating tactics to achieve those results. If a destructive leader is seen as a role model for their followers, they will convey the message that the negative behaviour is appropriate, creating an organisational culture that is permissive of destructive behaviours, where individuals will be rewarded solely for achieving their goals, despite the destruction and demoralisation of colleagues and employees caused along the way (Schyns & Schilling, 2013; Tepper, 2000, 2007). As a result, those who report to such leaders may adopt the same attitude towards the people they work with, driving them to produce the results demanded, and thereby creating a toxic work environment for their own teams. If there is no policy against abusive tactics, no monitoring of and no punishment for destructive behaviours, the organisation is seen to accept destructive leadership as a legitimate leadership style. Managers are then promoted, even when they have been engaging in manipulative or harmful behaviours towards others. When there are no useful checks and balances to guard against destructive practices, a prospective perpetrator will perceive the costs and dangers of engaging in unethical or destructive behaviour as very low (Daniel, 2017).

There is some evidence to suggest that feelings of organisational injustice resulting from observing or being a target of abusive supervision may lead to a reduction in organisational citizen behaviours by employees. In addition, the work stress resulting from abusive treatment by their manager may deplete an individual's resources to such an extent that they are unable to refrain from engaging in counterproductive work behaviours (Zhang, Liu, Xu, Yang & Bednall, 2019). This also has significant negative repercussions for an organisation's culture.

Impact on organisational performance

As noted above, in some circumstances, bullying and abusive behaviours can drive employees to achieve high levels of performance and to reach legitimate organisational goals. As a result, destructive leaders can be viewed as successful, even while harming their employees. Alternatively, destructive leaders who pursue goals that conflict with the organisation's interests (destructive goals) create conflicts in goal direction and a dysfunctional political environment. Pursuing destructive goals diverts organisational resources away from pursuing legitimate goals, resulting in progress on legitimate goals being delayed, thwarted or blocked. Where leaders coerce their followers to pursue destructive goals, they place the organisation at risk by aligning the organisation with unethical or illegal activities, endangering the organisation's reputation. Employees who comply with the leader's demands may even risk being subjected to legal action for following orders. The organisation then has to balance the needs of addressing the fallout from a leader's unethical or illegal behaviour with protecting followers from the consequences of their compliance (Krasikov et al., 2013).

High levels of terminations due to ethical violations or resignations due to destructive leadership also create disruption to performance. These events cause upheaval for management and employees, such as dealing with rumours and gossip and working out what will happen next. Replacement leaders may wish to come in with a 'new broom', promoting their own views of how things should be done, creating more conflict and negative emotions for those affected. This results in a lack of productivity among those who choose to stay and more disruption when many subsequently decide to leave (Daniel, 2017). Ultimately, self-oriented leaders will be unlikely to promote staff, customer and supplier interests or to engage in long-range planning, which in turn reduces an organisation's ability to achieve success.

Financial costs

It is difficult to specify the direct financial costs of destructive leadership, but the resultant stress, disengagement, withdrawal, presenteeism and absenteeism costs have been estimated. Costs to organisations as a result of the impact of work stressors, such as destructive leadership, are significant. Occupational stress is a major public health problem in Australia, costing the economy up to AU$15 billion per annum, with mental stress claims in Australia totalling approximately AU$543 million per annum (Brough, Raper & Spedding, 2020; Safe Work Australia, 2013, 2015). Lost productivity and absenteeism attributed to physical and mental health issues arising from occupational stress costs Australian organisations approximately AU$5 billion per annum (Price Waterhouse Coopers, 2014). Substantial litigation and counselling costs may be incurred to address the effects of hostility, bullying, discrimination, intimidation and abuse (Sutton, 2007). Even when it is recognised that a leader is engaging in unethical or illegal behaviour, the cost of resisting their influence or addressing their bad behaviour (e.g., legal action, escalated conflict and aggression, retaliatory action) can be perceived to be greater than the cost of not addressing the consequences of destructive behaviour (e.g., stress claims from affected employees).

Workers' compensation claims focusing on psychosocial injuries have increased over the past decade. Mental stress claims (e.g., stressful interpersonal relationships at work, social or physical isolation, poor relationships with superiors, interpersonal conflict, lack of social support, bullying and harassment) form a significant proportion of accepted workers' compensation claims in Australia and are the most expensive form of workers' compensation claim due to the typically lengthy periods of absence from work (Brough et al., 2020). If a worker is successful in their claim for workers' compensation for a psychological injury, no order will be made against an employer or the perpetrators of the abuse. Workers' compensation is solely concerned with providing workers with financial compensation, which in turn leads to higher premiums for the organisation.

There are also hidden costs incurred as a result of destructive leadership that are difficult to calculate – for example, costs resulting from high staff turnover (such as re-staffing and re-training), the affected employee reciprocating the negative treatment or employees withholding voluntary contributions that might benefit their supervisor or the organisation (Rafferty & Restubog, 2011). Gallup (2020) research reported that active disengagement, caused in part by managers' destructive behaviour, costs the USA an estimated $605 billion annually in lost productivity.

IMPLICATIONS FOR PRACTICE

The impact of destructive leadership requires early detection and intervention. The research is clear that protecting employees from the impact of destructive leadership saves substantial costs to organisations and to society. A review of the harmful consequences of destructive leadership reinforces the need to screen candidates with destructive tendencies, including leaders with narcissistic or psychopathic tendencies, from appointment to leadership positions. Executives and human resource professionals should be aware of the indicators of destructive leadership at individual, team, departmental and executive levels. Such indicators include poor organisational survey results, higher use of employee assistance programmes and increased rates of employee absenteeism, stress leave and turnover. Once a concern has been identified and investigated, clear policies and procedures must be followed to address destructive behaviours or even remove the perpetrators from the organisation. Studies have shown that often employees perceive that nothing happens to those responsible for the destructive behaviours (Brough, Lawrence, Tsahuridu & Brown, in press). Some report that such leaders are even promoted (Webster et al., 2016). Therefore, it is essential that executive and senior management are seen to be directly and effectively dealing with the destructive leadership.

CONCLUSION

Destructive leadership leads to a range of negative consequences for the leaders themselves, individual targets, teams and organisations. As discussed in this chapter, the impact of destructive leadership includes leader derailment, reduced individual and team performance, reduced employee satisfaction, commitment and wellbeing, increased psychological distress, absenteeism, unwanted turnover and occupational stress (mental health injury) claims. In addition, perceptions of abusive treatment by a leader may lead to retaliatory responses and an increase in counterproductive work behaviours, creating a toxic work environment. It is important to be able to identify and intervene early when incidents of destructive leadership are suspected. It is also important to understand the organisational cultures that provide a conducive environment for destructive leadership to flourish.

5

TOXIC ENVIRONMENTS: THE ROLE OF CULTURE

CHAPTER OVERVIEW

This chapter discusses the key organisational cultural factors that contribute to the prevalence of destructive leadership. First, we discuss how most organisational cultures are heterogeneous, consisting of a central formal culture and local worksite cultures that can differ significantly. For most employees, their local worksite cultures are the most influential, especially if these are managed by an abusive leader. We discuss the tangible and intangible aspects of the work cultures that both senior and local leaders commonly influence, and the four common styles of destructive leadership they utilise. Finally, we discuss the specific features of an organisational culture that are most commonly associated with toxic leadership, including a high power-distance and a 'masculinity contest' culture. We also identify how an organisation's level of ethical culture and procedural justice discourages destructive leadership and encourages employee reporting.

THE HETEROGENEITY OF ORGANISATIONAL CULTURE

The culture of an organisation is composed of the rules and standards of behaviour, both formal and informal, that are considered to be acceptable. Organisational culture can be formally defined by policies and practices, including guidance on unacceptable behaviours such as bullying and harassment. Of more influence, however, is the culture formed by workers' daily interactions, which may include variations of the 'formal' standard of conduct. New employees usually know to wait and observe the culture, to gain an informed understanding of exactly 'how things are done around here'. This experience may well differ from the formal learnings of the organisation's processes and systems experienced during recruitment, onboarding and training.

The importance of 'local' cultures within workplaces is also highly pertinent. Thus, the culture of an individual hospital ward or work team or police station may vary markedly from the environments of other wards or teams or police stations in the same organisation, as well as from the formal 'high level' organisational culture. These 'local' variations in organisational culture are often overlooked in research studies, primarily because a single homogenous organisational culture is considerably easier to assess and analyse. This is unfortunate, as local variations at specific worksites can contribute markedly to a worker's experiences and, indeed, to their work performance outcomes. Typically, the senior executive management team contributes the largest influence to the establishment of the central formal work culture, while the worksite leader significantly influences the localised worksite-specific culture.

IMPACT OF LEADERS AND SUPERVISORS ON ORGANISATIONAL CULTURE

Both the research evidence and most workers' own experiences demonstrate the significant impact that both local supervisors and senior leaders have on the culture of an organisation. Obviously, this impact can be both positive and negative. However, estimates indicate that up to 75% of employees have experienced negative behaviours from their managers (Hogan, Raskin & Fazzini, 1990), while the majority of occupational mental health stress claims are caused by adverse interpersonal workplace conflicts, including 'toxic leadership', as we discussed earlier (Webster, Brough & Daly, 2016). It is pertinent to consider *what* exactly is being influenced by these leaders. Both senior and local leaders can influence *tangible* aspects of an employee's working environment, including, for example, the dress code (e.g., the level of formality of work wear, casual wear on Fridays), the hours of work (e.g., an informal culture of long work hours), taking of leave (whether taking leave is a regular practice or is informally frowned upon), work–life balance (whether using work–life balance policies is encouraged or discouraged) and even how lunch is usually eaten (whether as a break from work or at desks while working; e.g., Brough, Timms, Chan, Hawkes & Rasmussen, 2020).

Intangible aspects of the working environment are also influenced by both senior and local leaders. These include, for example, the acceptable levels of behaviour, ranging from how service and administrative staff are treated (are they greeted and acknowledged or ignored?) to the degree to which objectionable behaviours are accepted (e.g., language, humour and behaviours based on derogatory content). The diversity of staff appointed to, and promoted within, an organisation is also another intangible feature of the organisational culture. Here we refer to diversity in terms of personal characteristics (skin colour, gender, sexuality), qualifications (levels obtained, place of education), personality traits (informed by psychometric testing) and even personal cognitions (opinions, ways of thinking). An organisation's culture thus has a substantial influence on the diversity (or lack of diversity) of its staff, and this explains, for example, why some conservative organisations continue to employ and promote primarily white male employees (Brough, Brown & Biggs, 2016).

A key intangible aspect of the working-environment impact that is influenced by both local and senior leaders is the 'safety' and tone of the psychological working environment (Dollard, Shimazu, Bin Nordin, Brough & Tuckey, 2014). This includes the methods by which employees are managed and supervised, and especially the interactions between managers and their staff. The rest of this chapter discusses the factors of organisational culture that provide a conducive environment for the occurrence of destructive leadership. We focus on three common factors of organisational culture that contribute to destructive leadership: style of leadership, power-distance between leaders and followers and a lack of governance and cultural norms (Mulvey & Padilla, 2010).

ORGANISATIONAL CULTURE FACTORS THAT ENCOURAGE DESTRUCTIVE LEADERSHIP

Style of leadership

How a manager chooses to supervise and interact with their staff is obviously a key factor for the demonstration of destructive leadership behaviours. The extent to which negative leadership behaviours are tolerated within the organisation is highly dependent on the organisation's culture and especially on the opinions of the senior leaders. Thus, a 'bullying' culture can certainly exist, whereby destructive leadership flows down from senior executives and is informally reinforced within an organisation. The specific style of leadership most commonly associated with destructive leadership has been formally investigated within the research literature. One pertinent study assessed five key types of destructive leadership to identify the most commonly employed, categorised on two axes consisting of the organisation and its subordinates (Aasland, Skogstad, Notelaers, Nielsen & Einarsen, 2010). This work also expands on Einarsen, Aasland and Skogstad's (2007) destructive leadership model discussed in Chapter 2 of this book.

In their research, Aasland et al. (2010) reported that *laissez-faire* leadership behaviour was the most prevalent and sits in the middle of the organisation–subordinate axis. *Supportive–disloyal* leadership is classified as pro-subordinate and anti-organisation, while *derailed* leadership is classified as both anti-subordinate and anti-organisation. Compared to *constructive* leadership, which is both pro-subordinate and pro-organisation, *tyrannical* leadership behaviour is classified as anti-subordinate and pro-organisation and was the least prevalent. Importantly, the research participants reported experiencing *all forms* of destructive leadership behaviours at various times; thus, bad leaders typically employ a variety of these destructive leadership styles. We discussed these types of leadership in detail in a previous chapter, so we include just brief summaries of these negative leadership styles here.

Laissez-faire leadership describes a passive method of leadership, by which leadership responsibilities are avoided. Laissez-faire leadership behaviours include a lack of decision-making, initiative, goal attainment and concern for subordinates. Laissez-faire leadership behaviours are primarily caused by the leader's lack of motivation, knowledge or competence, as well as an intent to cause harm.

Supportive–disloyal leadership is characterised by behaviours supportive of their subordinates but negative to the organisation. These managers typically over-compensate their staff in support, resources, low workloads and encourage their counterproductive workplace behaviours, at the expense of the organisation. Such counterproductive workplace behaviours may include, for example, theft, fraud and embezzlement: the 'dirty cop' style of leadership. Thus, support and camaraderie with their subordinates is high, with no negative interpersonal interactions. However, appropriate positive leadership is absent, and the encouragement of counterproductive workplace behaviours characterises the 'destructive' element of this leadership style.

A **derailed leadership** style is described by Aasland et al. (2010) as displaying negative behaviours to both subordinates and the organisation. A derailed leader is the classic workplace bully, repeatedly humiliating and manipulating their subordinates, while also committing theft or fraud or demonstrating a lack of performance towards the organisation. The primary focus of a derailed leader is personal gain.

Finally, **tyrannical leadership** is defined in Aasland et al.'s (2010) model as being supportive to the organisation but anti-subordinate. Tyrannical leaders behave in a similar way towards their staff as do derailed leaders – that is, bullying and manipulating their subordinates. However, tyrannical leaders display positive performance management to their superiors, including a strong focus of goal attainment, so their superiors usually have a positive impression of them – quite the opposite view compared to this type of leader's subordinates.

HIERARCHICAL AND MASCULINE ORGANISATION STRUCTURES

The hierarchical structure of an organisation has also been associated with a higher prevalence of destructive leadership experiences (e.g., Maner & Mead, 2010; Spangler, Tikhomirov, Sotak & Palrecha, 2014; Tepper, 2007). The presence of ranks, a power-distance between leaders and followers (i.e., chain of command), lack of transparency in management decision-making and closed communication channels all characterise hierarchical organisations which are commonly associated with frequent occurrences of abusive leadership. These highly structured organisations have also been referred to as 'win or die' cultures and 'masculinity contest cultures' (Berdahl, Cooper, Glick, Livingston & Williams, 2018; Matos, O'Neill & Lei, 2018). Berdahl et al. (2018) describe how in masculinity contest cultures, abusive supervision and counterproductive workplace behaviours are covertly displayed and informally encouraged in order to secure career advancements. Organisations characterised by masculinity contest cultures have a focus on employee personal gain and advancement at the expense of other employees and hence adopt a 'mine's bigger than yours' contest for workloads, work hours, risk-taking and organisational resources – including, for example, the most/best office space, parking space, administrative support, internal development funds, etc. (Brough, Wall & Cooper, 2021).

Berdahl et al. (2018, p. 431) describe how in masculinity contest cultures, 'men and women alike must play the game to survive or win'. Importantly, the masculinity contest cultures do not refer only to gender but also to an employee's race and sexuality, and they also include, to a lesser extent, other individual characteristics such as class, education and religion. White, heterosexual males are typically the 'dominant' players within these organisations. These hierarchical masculinity contest cultures are most prevalent in medicine, finance, engineering, law, politics, sports, police, fire, corrections and military services and tech organisations; see, for example, Rawski and Workman-Stark's (2018) account of the consequences of a masculinity contest culture within some police services.

Hierarchical masculinity contest cultures explain the lack of diversity of employees in senior leadership positions, which, as we noted at the beginning of this chapter, works to reinforce the continuation of the organisation's dominant conservative, white, male culture. Matos et al. (2018) also reported a strong positive association between an organisation's masculinity contest cultures and the occurrence of toxic leadership behaviours. This includes, for example, supervisors taking the credit for their staff's success and blaming staff for their failures. Matos et al. (2018) found that employees of organisations with masculinity contest cultures reported high levels of occupational stress and turnover intentions and low levels of work–life balance. However, male employees also reported higher level of work engagement and commitment, compared to female employees; this indicates why (male) employees are retained within these work cultures.

Padilla, Hogan and Kaiser (2007) summarised the triadic influence of supervisors, followers and work cultures in the experience of toxic leadership within their 'toxic triangle' model. This model was influential in moving the discussion of toxic leaders away from their individual characteristics, to instead emphasise a *system perspective* of how individuals and their organisational environments combine to generate toxic leaders. This toxic triangle model is pertinent for acknowledging both the positive and negative impact of destructive leaders, the common characteristics of followers that enable destructive leaders and, importantly, organisational features such as culture and instability that enhance a destructive leader's impact. Specifically, Padilla et al. (2007) described the key organisational cultural values associated with the occurrence of destructive leaders as consisting of collectivism (promoting high levels of loyalty and group identity among employees), high power-distance (hierarchical power structures) and avoidance of uncertainty (low risk-taking, high security).

ORGANISATIONAL ETHICAL CULTURE

The absence of appropriate organisational ethical systems (i.e., checks and balances) is also a feature of the cultural environment that is conducive to destructive leadership, as noted in Padilla et al.'s (2007) toxic triangle model. In the absence of appropriate control systems, it is obviously easier for leaders to abuse their power and positions. Leaders with unilateral control are more likely to exhibit destructive leadership behaviours towards their followers, as well as commit theft and fraud in their organisation. New and small high-transformative organisations, especially those with highly charismatic leaders, are less likely to have appropriate management systems in place to prevent such leadership power abuses. Thus, these new, small organisations are more susceptible to the occurrence of these aversive leaders (Mulvey & Padilla, 2010).

The influence of an organisation's ethical culture and climate upon the behaviours of its workers at all levels has long been established (e.g., Kaptein, 2011; Schwartz, 2016; Victor & Cullen, 1988). Thus, an organisation's moral code of conduct influences employees' behaviours, including the occurrence of abusive leadership. Zhou, Liu, Chen and Zhao (2018), for example, demonstrated that employees who considered their organisation to have a strong ethical climate had a greater sense of belonging and attachment to the organisation (i.e., identification), and this in turn increased their likeliness to report any inappropriate behaviours. Similar reasoning occurs for the perceived level of organisational justice and procedural justice inherent within an organisation (Greenberg, 1990; Ugaddan & Park, 2019), which both serve to increase employees' reporting behaviours during the occurrence of adverse or fraudulent behaviours. Thus, reporting behaviours are likely to occur when employees perceive they will be believed and that action will be taken to stop and resolve the reported bad behaviours.

IMPLICATIONS FOR PRACTICE

Leadership development programmes and interventions targeted at improving leadership characteristics have a limited impact when considered in isolation from the prevailing worksite and/or the broader organisational culture. The success of leadership programmes – that is, the immediate transfer of training to long-term adoption of constructive leadership styles, mindsets and behaviours – is significantly influenced by the prevailing culture. For practitioners aiming to identify and address destructive leadership in their organisation, consideration can be given to the effectiveness of the checks and balances that have been put in place and to the environmental influences and cultural enablers within the organisation that lead to a tolerance for and reinforcement of destructive behaviours by managers.

CONCLUSION

In this chapter, we have discussed the key features of an organisation's culture that increase the likelihood of destructive leadership behaviours. We have described the occurrence of both central formal cultures and the local worksite cultures that often have a greater impact on employees' behaviours and experiences. We have also discussed both the tangible and intangible components of organisational culture that are most likely to be influenced by our work leaders, from the degree of employee diversity to expected work hours. We have identified the four common types of destructive leadership described by Aasland et al. (2010) and noted that laissez-faire leadership behaviour is the most prevalent. Finally, we have discussed the specific features of an organisational culture that are most commonly associated with toxic leadership. These features include a high power-distance and a masculinity contest culture commonly found within hierarchical organisation structures. We have also noted how a strong organisational ethical culture and a perceived high level of procedural justice serve to discourage inappropriate work behaviours and to encourage employee reporting.

However, we acknowledge that almost regardless of an organisation's level of ethical climate and hierarchical structure, the formal reporting of their own supervisor remains a substantial hurdle for many workers. In the next chapter, we discuss the common reasons why employees *don't* report their supervisors and instead prefer to remain silent about the abusive behaviours they experience.

6

ORGANISATIONAL AND EMPLOYEE SILENCE

CHAPTER OVERVIEW

This chapter discusses two common impacts of destructive leadership: employee silence and organisational silence. We first focus on employee silence and discuss how this silence is the common reaction to experienced or observed destructive leadership behaviours and how it is motivated by an employee's fear of retaliation from either their manager or colleagues. The chapter describes how a multi-level approach is most effective for reducing employee silence, increasing employee voice and reducing the occurrence of destructive leadership behaviours. This multi-level approach consists of key individual employee characteristics, managers' characteristics, the organisational context and the national culture and legislation, which combine to influence the occurrence and the reporting of destructive leadership behaviours. The chapter includes a case study about why employee whistleblowing should be considered as a positive form of employee voice for organisations. The chapter also discusses the broader concept of organisational silence and its associated adverse consequences for both workers and organisations. Finally, we identify how strong ethical leadership by senior managers is essential to produce reductions in the occurrence of both employee and organisational silence and to support employees who do find their voice and formally report destructive leadership behaviours.

EMPLOYEE SILENCE

It is clear that one common consequence of destructive leadership is the formal lack of acknowledgement of the issue by those who experience it – namely, *employee silence*. Chapters 4 and 5 discussed the common impacts of destructive leadership upon employees and the organisation and how a negative organisational culture acts to perpetrate the occurrence of destructive leadership. These chapters identified common reasons why employees do not confront destructive leaders, and these organisational, cultural and power differential issues can also produce a lack of acknowledgement or *silence* from exposed employees and observers. Employee silence is defined as an employee intentionally withholding ideas, information, concerns and opinions about issues related to their job and the organisation (Dyne, Ang & Botero, 2003). Indeed, Rai and Agarwal (2018, p. 227) identified employee silence as '*one of the most significant passive responses that employees display in the face of mistreatment at work*'. Clearly, affected employees are often too intimidated, ashamed or concerned about the consequences to raise the issue of destructive leadership, and this silence often spills over to impact multiple facets of their job and wellbeing.

Employee silence is widespread. Locke and Anderson (2015) studied employee silence across multiple industry sectors and noted that approximately 85% of employees felt unable to raise a critical work issue with their manager and, importantly, 70% of employees stayed silent when their manager made an obvious mistake. This frequency of employee silence in the face of critical work errors largely explains why workplace embezzlements, accidents and fatalities occur, especially within the hierarchically structured finance, health and transport industries. A form of employee silence based specifically on the supervisor–subordinate relationship was described by Brinsfield (2013). Brinsfield suggested that it is important to understand the specific motives that employees have to stay silent in the face of supervisor misbehaviour. Understanding these motives can improve solutions to overcome this silence and instead provide employees with the confidence to voice their concerns. Brinsfield (2013) identified six categories of employee silence:

1. *deviant silence* defined as withholding some essential information,

2. *relational silence* based on a preference to not damage the supervisor–subordinate relationship,

3. *defensive silence* motivated by fear and self-protection,

4. *diffident silence* based on self-doubt and a lack of confidence,

5. *ineffectual silence* involving resignation and acceptance of the circumstances and

6. *disengaged silence* motivated by a general lack of concern about the issue.

In practice, we suggest that employee silence in the face of supervisors' destructive behaviours often incorporates many of these forms of silence. Thus, employees may feel disengaged because they believe voicing their concerns will not result in any change, they may feel resigned to the issue continuing or they may not wish to make the relationships with their supervisor any worse, and so they may withhold information about their supervisor's toxic behaviours.

REASONS FOR EMPLOYEE SILENCE

Retaliation

Both Wortley, Cassematis and Donkin (2008) and Webster, Brough and Daly (2016) reported that the anticipated adverse reaction of management was the most common reason for employee silence, with more than one third of employees believing that any submitted report or grievance would be ignored and that they would suffer retaliation as a consequence. Similarly, a comparison of international workers who had submitted a formal organisational wrongdoing report found that 38% of US employees and 22% of Australian employees had experienced subsequent retaliation, compared to only 4% of the Norwegian sample (Miceli & Near, 2013). The most common retaliation mistreatments reported by employees include demotions, reprisals, negative performance appraisals, harassment, isolation, expulsion, suspension and poor mental and physical health outcomes (Brough, Lawrence, Tsahuridu, & Brown, in press).

This fear of retaliation remains the key reason why employee silence still frequently occurs and is primarily due to the inequitable power relationship between the supervisor and employee. Thus, the worker is primarily reliant on their supervisor for employment, resources and career advancement, and employees fear that these resources may be withheld from them in the future. Maintaining their silence, therefore, is a method for employees to retain these current and future resources (Rai & Agarwal, 2018) and this acts as a strong motivation to keep silent. Clearly, there is a strong relationship between a leader's destructive personality and employee silence, primarily based on this fear of retaliation mistreatment (Song, Qian, Wang, Yang & Zhai, 2017). The worker may also perceive that senior management will not support any formal grievance or bullying reports against their supervisor, even when aware of formal organisational anti-bullying policies. This is especially common if the supervisor is successful at impression management with their senior managers, as we discussed in Chapter 2.

Lack of impact

Another primary reason for employee silence is a perception that nothing will change after a report is made. This perception is strongly influenced by the organisational culture, as we discussed in Chapter 5. Thus, if the organisational culture is based on mistrust, inequity and bullying at all levels, including senior leader levels, then an employee will understandably perceive that their formal reporting of misbehaviour will achieve minimal senior management support and will consequently produce few changes. Conversely, organisations exhibiting a supportive, ethical culture and a high degree of trust between workers and managers are more likely to receive employee reports of a manager's destructive behaviours, as well as other reports of manager wrongdoing (Brough, Lawrence, Tsahuridu, & Brown, in press).

National context

The impact of a national context is also important in an employee's decision to maintain their silence or not. This includes a country's cultural power orientation, where, for example, obedience and acquiescence to supervisors may be highly acceptable and, thus, any questioning of supervisors is frowned upon. Indeed, the rudimentary acknowledgement that destructive leadership behaviours have actually occurred is less likely to be identified in countries with a high power-orientation culture (Lian, Ferris & Brown, 2012). Multiple studies of the occurrence of leaders' destructive behaviours and bullying of employees based in such countries as India, China and Japan have demonstrated how this deferential national culture is highly influential for the occurrence of employee silence (Gupta, Bakhshi & Einarsen, 2017). This power orientation is also compounded by gender. Female employees within high power-orientation countries are typically more likely to experience workplace bullying and destructive leadership behaviours but *less* likely to formally report such experiences (Rai & Agarwal, 2018).

Similarly, the national legislative context also influences the occurrence of employee silence – in particular, legislature relating to employee health and wellbeing – and reporting internal organisational wrongdoings – that is, whistle-blowing. In some countries, for example, this legislation is applied differently for private- and public-sector workers. Countries formally adopting anti-retaliation legislation (e.g., Australia, New Zealand, USA, UK) support the protection of employees who submit reports of organisational wrongdoing, including reports of bullying and harassment (Brough, Lawrence, Tsahuridu, & Brown, in press). In contrast, other countries adopt perspectives where employee protection is not emphasised. For example, in Germany, an employee's perceived disloyalty to an employer is legally upheld and can result in the dismissal of employees who formally report organisational wrongdoing (Forst, 2013). It is therefore clear that employee silence and the perpetration of destructive leadership behaviours is influenced by numerous factors internal and external to an organisation – namely, the seriousness and consequences of the destructive behaviours, the employee–supervisor relationship, specific national legislative frameworks, employee protections and national norms/cultures.

Individual characteristics

Finally, the individual characteristics of the employee and how these character-istics influence their decision to stay silent or to report destructive leadership behaviours are also relevant to consider. These key characteristics include the employee's seniority and tenure with the organisation, ethical training and moral efficacy, willingness to submit a formal report, psychosocial job characteristics (i.e., workload, support and control; Brough, Drummond & Biggs, 2018) and their personality and demographic characteristics (Brough, Lawrence, Tsahuridu, & Brown, in press). These key characteristics are directly associated with the employee's decision to submit a formal report, which in turn results in their involvement with the investigation and their experi-enced degree of support. The degree of stress experienced by an employee also influences whether they maintain their silence about their manager's destructive behaviours. The fear of adding more stress to an already high load and/or a lack of energy to drive any reporting for employees experienc-ing high levels of emotional exhaustion also contribute to their inaction and their silence (Xu, Loi & Lam, 2015).

Overcoming employee silence and producing a cessation or a positive change in these adverse supervisory behaviours is obviously crucial. The importance of increasing employees' courage and their voice in these sit-uations has been widely recognised and defined as reporting behaviours undertaken despite a high level of fear of the consequences (Jones & Kelly, 2014; Kilmann, O'Hara & Strauss, 2013). Indeed, employee voice has been strongly associated with employee wellbeing and work performance. Employee voice is formally defined as a critical mechanism for employees to improve working conditions and enable them to change situations which may lead them to feel exhausted or to withdraw from the workplace (Brooks & Wilkinson, in press). It is apparent that multiple factors impact employee silence in the face of destructive leadership behaviours. Solutions that consider these multiple factors and the interactions between them are the most likely to succeed in addressing employee silence. We summarise these key factors in Figure 6.1. We suggest this is a useful framework for consideration in future research focused on addressing destructive leadership and reducing employee silence.

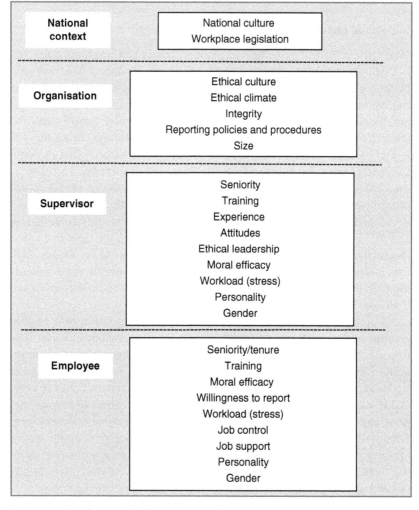

Figure 6.1   Multi-level model of key factors to address employee silence.

CASE STUDY: EMPLOYEES WHO BLOW THE WHISTLE

Not all formal reports of whistleblowing concern destructive leadership, but a high proportion (approximately 80%) of whistleblowing reports are based on leadership bullying and other toxic behaviours. These high rates of workplace bullying and harassment are directly associated with workplace health and safety injury (stress) claims (Brough, Raper & Spedding, 2020; Webster et al., 2016). We recently conducted stage two of the 'Whistling while you work' research project, which collected whistleblowing experiences from employee reporters, managers and human resource/policy officers in 699 public, private and not-for-profit organisations throughout Australia and New Zealand (Brown et al., 2019). This project identified how effective organisational whistleblowing processes are vital for organisational integrity and good governance. Thus, it is highly preferable for organisations to receive reports of any wrongdoing internally from their employees and act to remedy such wrongdoing, rather than obstruct internal reporting so that reports are forced to be made externally to crime and misconduct government agencies and/or to the media. Indeed, this recognition is driving such agencies as the European Union to issue new legal whistleblowing reforms for its member states. The International Standards Organisation (ISO) is also developing the world's first whistleblowing management system standard (Brown et al., 2019).

This whistleblowing project surveyed 17,778 individual respondents who had reported or managed an internal whistleblowing report or who had overseen whistleblowing policies in these organisations (governance professionals). The results indicated that employees who witnessed or experienced wrongdoing stayed silent in approximately 30% of incidents. For employees who did report an incident, approximately 37% identified that wrongdoing was found and internally dealt with as a result of their reports. Just over half (56%) of managers and governance professionals identified that a formal report had been dealt with and had impacted some type of organisational change (Brown et al., 2019). While these figures may exclude reporters or managers who were *not aware* of any consequential action being taken on receipt of a report, these figures are still surprisingly low and suggest that either little action actually occurs or that the reporters/managers are not informed about the direct consequences of a submitted report. These figures clearly require improvement, especially if the internal reporting of wrongdoing is to be encouraged. The project concluded that '[d]ealing with employee wrongdoing concerns may be challenging and difficult, but our research confirms its fundamental role, every day, in maintaining integrity and assisting accountability and performance in the institutions on which society depends' (Brown et al., 2019, p. 15).

Approximately 41% of submitted reports resulted in a positive conse-quence. This commonly included disciplinary action for the wrongdoer, training, personnel or structural changes, changed policies and procedures and remedial actions such as apologies or compensation to the reporters or victims. However, over half (54%) of reporters had been treated badly by their management or colleagues. Common forms of adverse treatment experienced by employees after formally reporting an incident include stress caused by the internal investigative process, work performance disruptions and reductions, isolation, ostracism and harassment by colleagues and/or managers, denial of career advancement (promotions, training, bonuses), negative performance appraisal, reassignment to less desirable duties or locations, demotion or suspension, denial of job resources, dismissal and disciplinary or legal action (Brown et al., 2019).

The project noted that in many cases, formal acknowledgement by the organisation of the employee's voice and bravery in reporting would likely have prevented many of the adverse repercussions that the reporter had expe-rienced from their colleagues and managers. Organisations have a clear duty to support and protect reporters from repercussions and reprisals and, impor-tantly, organisations should proactively and publicly address these risks to their employees. One organisational factor that protected reporters from reprisals was the occurrence of *strong ethical leadership* by senior managers – that is, if senior managers communicated the importance of ethics and integrity clearly and convincingly and set a good example. Consequently, as we noted above, there has been recent interest in the provision of ethical leadership training to managers at all levels. This training, combined with appropriate formal organ-isational policies, directly assists in the *prevention* of destructive leadership behaviours and *protects* employees after reporting such behaviours (Brough, Lawrence, Tsahuridu, & Brown, in press). The whistleblowing project noted that '[f]ar from being a mere "feel good" factor in the style and rhetoric of managers, senior management ethical leadership and behaviour reinforcement are critical to an environment in which support flows, and good investigation outcomes and benefits are achieved' (Brown et al., 2019, p. 38).

ORGANISATIONAL SILENCE

Organisational silence describes a *collective* level of silence, in contrast to indi-vidual employee silence, discussed above. Formally, organisational silence is defined as 'a phenomenon in which an organization's employees refuse to state their views on organizational affairs for various reasons' (Akar, 2018, p. 1078).

However, organisational silence is usually understood to have a broader reach beyond a simple lack of voice and includes, for example, workers' collective disengagement with the work environment, their negative attitudes, disagreement and withdrawal behaviours (Nafei, 2016). Pope (2019) observed that organisational silence is not a characteristic of a healthy institution, but one of the outward signs of an organisation which is hiding and retreating from reality.

Employee silence does not on its own create a culture of organisational silence, but a widespread organisational environment of silence certainly reinforces employees' silence. Organisational silence is elicited by core organisational characteristics, conditions and processes that work directly and indirectly to produce a widespread culture of silence and suppression. Such organisational characteristics include, for example, formal hierarchical power dynamics and institutional structures that create and sustain silence as a means to neutralise the perceived threat of employee voice (Morrison, 2014; Morrison & Milliken, 2000). Organisational disregard for concerns that are raised by employees, including a lack of action or consequence arising from formal reports, serves to reinforce a climate of organisational silence (Jones & Kelly, 2014; Webster et al., 2016).

Similar to employee silence, organisational silence is fundamentally based on the erroneous perception that any worker feedback will be negative and counterproductive to a manager's or to the organisation's performance. Thus, workers' feedback is avoided and is actively supressed. Workers remain silent due to a fear of negative repercussions. Organisational silence is therefore typically related to low perceptions of trust and justice in an organisation. While the lack of any negative feedback may be perceived as a positive situation, in reality, organisational silence actively prevents an organisation from adapting and developing, innovation is minimal and any organisational decision-making is usually ineffective (Akar, 2018). Organisational silence is also directly associated with adverse worker attitudes, such as low levels of work engagement, job commitment and job satisfaction and high levels of turnover. Organisations with high levels of organisational silence commonly report high levels of other adverse behaviours and consequences for their workers, including occurrences of bullying and harassment, high stress and burnout and unethical work practices.

Interestingly, many of the research studies assessing organisational silence have been conducted in the healthcare (e.g., hospitals) and education (e.g., universities) industries and typically focus on (the absence of) fair and equitable employment practices and the high levels of formal administration within these sectors (Akar, 2018). For example, one recent assessment of the occurrence of organisational silence within the UK's National Health Service (NHS) described the context as follows: 'the NHS is systemically and institutionally deaf, bullying, defensive and dishonest. There appears to be a culture of fear, lack of voice and silence. The cost of suppression of voice, reluctance to voice and the resulting "sea of silence" is immense. There is a resistance to "knowing" and the NHS appears to be hiding and retreating from reality. There is an urgent need for action to be taken to address this dysfunctional culture' (Pope, 2019, p. 45). Pope (2019) suggested three key explanations of why the NHS was experiencing such 'organisational dysfunction': protection of its image, organisational silence and normalised organisational corruption. Given the more recent consequences of COVID-19 impacting the NHS (and other health services), it would be highly pertinent to assess in what ways this description of organisational silence within the NHS has now changed – for the better or worse.

REDUCING THE OCCURRENCE OF ORGANISATIONAL SILENCE

Similar to the ways by which employee silence can be reduced, effectively decreasing levels of organisational silence and promoting employee voice require a multi-method proactive approach by all levels of managers. Most commonly, an organisational cultural change is usually required, with effective channels of communication introduced between workers and both their direct supervisors and more senior managers. Methods to build trust between workers and these managers are essential, and this usually requires a change in the managers' leadership styles. Organisational silence is negatively associated with transformational leadership behaviours, so an effective way to *reduce* organisational silence is to appoint a transformational leader to a department or to lead an organisation (Akar, 2018). As we discussed above, implementing overt ethical leadership practices, at both supervisor and senior manager levels, is crucial to increase workers' trust, voice and reporting behaviours. These required changes to reduce levels of organisational silence are, therefore, not at all quick and easy. Indeed, it has been observed that it may be difficult to restore that trust in a short period of time. This is because breaking silence and transitioning from a climate of silence to one that encourages talking may need a revolutionary or radical change of system (Nafei, 2016).

PRACTICAL IMPLICATIONS

Any serious attempts to improve organisational and employee silence must be initiated by the recognition that this form of worker suppression is occurring, that it has long-term disadvantages for the organisation and that a systematic change is necessary to improve the context. Typically, such recognition is best produced by an objective external body with expertise in organisational culture change. An effective way to produce the required systematic change is to appoint (or train) organisational leaders in ethical, democratic and transformational leadership behaviours. Typically, an overt leadership change (i.e., employing a different type of leader) brings with it the required cultural change and the associated improvements in organisational trust, justice and transparency, which are essential to reduce the context of organisational silence and to improve workers' willingness to speak up, report and engage with organisational practices and decision-making. Clear communication channels and a lack of reprisals must also be implemented to assist in any long-term positive culture change.

CONCLUSION

The personal or observed experience of destructive leadership behaviours commonly results in considerable employee distress and mistrust of the organisation. The frequent reaction of employees is to stay silent in this situation, in the hope that such behaviours will cease or to prevent the situation from escalating further. Different types of organisational and employee silence have been defined in an attempt to understand employees' specific motivations behind this silence and to encourage employees to have a voice in the face of wrongdoing. However, we suggest that a focus on the individual employee is not always useful. Instead, an understanding of the multiple levels that influence both the occurrence of these destructive leadership behaviours and its associated employee silence is recommended as being more useful in informing effective remedy or interventions. Thus, we have discussed how key individual employee characteristics, manager characteristics, the organisational context and the national culture and legislation all influence the occurrence and the reporting of destructive leadership behaviours. Such a comprehensive approach is required to influence any positive change and to provide employees with the suitable protection required for them to voice their adverse experiences.

We ended this chapter by discussing a case study developed from our 'Whistling while you work' research project. The case study illustrated how infrequently formal reports of wrongdoing (i.e., employee voice) actually occur and the adverse repercussions reporters commonly experienced. We have suggested that the need for *strong ethical leadership* by senior managers is essential for our organisations to produce reductions in the occurrence of organisational and employee silence and to support employees who do find their voice and formally report destructive leadership behaviours.

7

CONSEQUENCES OF DESTRUCTIVE LEADERSHIP FOR EMPLOYEES

CHAPTER OVERVIEW

The research is clear – destructive leadership leads to both short-term and long-term psychological, emotional, physical and career harm to employees. While the academic research refers to 'followers', the consequences of destructive leadership are felt by both targets and third-party observers. This chapter explores the mechanisms by which employees identify destructive leadership and the manager/employee dynamics that may increase or decrease the impact of the abuse.

EMPLOYEE HARM AS A CONSEQUENCE OF DESTRUCTIVE LEADERSHIP

Evidence clearly indicates that destructive leadership can be highly damaging for the wellbeing of those targeted. Common individual psychological impacts include self-doubt and feeling highly stressed, anxious and depressed. Emotional effects include feelings of mistrust, fear, anger, shame and emotional exhaustion. A range of physical health symptoms are also reported, including colds, gastric upsets, hair loss, skin rashes, headaches, high blood pressure and insomnia. Careers can be adversely affected by, for example, the leader damaging their targets' reputations, taking credit for the targets' good work or isolating targets from their social networks. Although the literature conceptualises destructive leadership as regularly exhibiting a number of harmful behaviours over time, for many individuals, significant harm was reported with just one perceived toxic behaviour from their manager (Holland, 2019; Schyns & Schilling, 2013; Webster, Brough & Daly, 2016).

Theoretical frameworks and research relevant to the negative impacts of destructive leadership on followers can be found in the occupational stress management literature. Destructive leadership behaviours form part of the psychosocial occupational stressor *anti-social behaviours*, which lead to anxiety, fear, depression and avoidance behaviours in affected individuals. Occupational stress impacts both wellbeing (i.e., the psychological, emotional and physical health of an employee) and their coping responses (i.e., efforts to prevent or reduce the negative effects of stress on wellbeing; Goh, Sawang & Oei, 2010). Individual factors (e.g., personality traits such as optimism) and situational factors (e.g., social support) have also been investigated for their role in influencing resilience through effective coping with stressful experiences such as destructive leadership.

Destructive leadership negatively impacts employees' work-related attitudes (i.e., job satisfaction, organisational commitment and intentions to quit), increases resistance behaviour (e.g., refusal to follow the leader's directions), increases anti-social and deviant behaviour (e.g., aggression and rudeness towards the leader and co-workers, counterproductive behaviours) and reduces performance, psychological wellbeing and family wellbeing (e.g., expressing displaced work-related resentment and anger towards family members, undermining family members or investing more energy and time at work than home to avoid repercussions from their manager). These effects are stronger for those who feel trapped and unable to escape from the abuse (Carlson, Ferguson, Hunter & Whitten, 2012; Mitchell & Ambrose, 2012; Tepper, Simon & Park, 2017).

One of the core reasons why destructive leadership is so harmful is that employees often don't realise they are the target until it is too late (Winn & Dykes, 2019). Hence, they may initially engage in ineffective coping mechanisms (we describe these in Chapter 8). Several inventories have been designed for individuals to rate their observations of harmful behaviours exhibited by their manager. Tepper (2000), for example, developed 15 abusive supervision items to assess followers' self-report observations of their supervisor's behaviour. Babiak and Hare (2007), Clarke (2005) and Lubit (2004) also provided sets of criteria to identify destructive leaders in organisations. Crowley and Elster (2009) provided a checklist of 20 behaviours for followers' reference to identify frustrating managerial behaviours. Table 7.1 compares four of these assessment instruments designed to be completed by followers/targets in order to identify if they are working for a destructive manager. While these diagnostic inventories may be of assistance to employees in determining whether they work for an abusive manager, they do not, of course, assist them with how to effectively respond to the abuse.

Table 7.1   Comparison of published inventories to identify destructive leaders.

Measure	Tepper (2000)	Lubit (2004)	Clarke (2005) and Babiak and Hare (2007)	Crowley and Elster (2009)
Subclinical psychopathy			•	
Narcissistic/ego-centred		•	•	•
Machiavellian/manipulative		•	•	•
Abusive supervision	•			
Emotionally volatile		•	•	•
Intimidating		•	•	•
Micromanaging/controlling		•		•
Paranoid		•	•	
Passive-aggressive		•		•
Unethical		•	•	•
Unpredictable		•	•	•

Harm occurs when employees' resources are inadequate to meet job demands. Destructive leadership leads to higher cognitive demands (e.g., pressure to quickly answer work-related messages or to problem solve when criticised) and higher emotional demands (e.g. maintaining a professional and positive demeanour at work when feeling anxious or stressed). High job demands can normally be reduced by workers attempting to improve their levels of task/job autonomy (i.e., control over the ways of working) and increasing support and resources from their manager. In the context of destructive leadership, autonomy is constrained by the manager and support is withheld, so the increased effort to meet job demands produces a chronic stress experience. The worker often finds it difficult to relax or detach psychologically from work and the abuse they experience. This extra effort and lack of recovery over the longer term leads to reduced job satisfaction and performance and ultimately emotional exhaustion and burnout (Brough, Drummond & Biggs, 2018).

COVID-19 has caused a major change in work circumstances, with many workers now regularly working from home (Chan, Shang, Brough, Wilkinson & Lu, 2021). Little research has assessed the consequences of destructive leadership for employees working remotely full-time or for those working a hybrid model, combining working from home and the office. It is clear that working from home for many has increased the volume of work they undertake within non-work hours. Some workers have also reported receiving excessive, unreasonable or unattainable requests from their managers, being expected to be constantly available for work and subjected to unethical monitoring by their manager (Chan et al., 2021; Dolce, Vayre, Molino & Ghislieri, 2020). Women may be more susceptible to trauma and exhaustion given that their double burden of work and family, especially when working from home, limits their chances of recovery (Brough, Kinman, McDowall & Chan, 2021; Dolce, Vayre, Molino & Ghislieri, 2020). It is also easier for a destructive leader to withhold important information and isolate employees from their colleagues when working in a virtual environment (He, Wu, Wu & Fu, 2021).

EMOTIONAL AND PSYCHOLOGICAL CONSEQUENCES OF DESTRUCTIVE LEADERSHIP

The emotions experienced by targets depend on how they interpret or appraise what is happening when experiencing abuse from their manager. For example, destructive leader behaviours can elicit fear through intimidation (e.g., yelling when a deadline is missed), anger through treating them unfairly (e.g., taking credit for their work) or shame through embarrassing them (e.g., hanging a 'wall of shame' board to advertise employees' blunders; Pelletier, 2010; Webster et al., 2016). Although negative emotions may arise from specific abusive events when they occur, generalised emotional states may evolve over time that are not clearly related to the original incidents (Peng, Schaubroeck, Chong & Li, 2019). Psychological consequences can arise from experiencing sustained negative emotions. Suppressed anger can subside into anxiety and depression (Pyc, Meltzer & Liu, 2017). Employees experiencing interpersonal stress, as a result of being in conflict with their manager and perhaps also their colleagues, are more likely to experience emotional exhaustion and burnout (Harms, Credé, Tynan, Leon & Jeung, 2017).

Fear

Fear is a fundamental emotion arising from a perception of threat and danger to self, especially when individuals perceive they cannot effectively cope with the situation. The leader's behaviour generates fear and a strong drive for self-protection in targets – that is, to avoid any actions that might lead to further abuse. Although abusive managers pose a threat that targets may wish to avoid, due to the power imbalance and the leader's powers to sanction, targets often feel constrained in how they respond and are left vulnerable to further abuse. In this context, abusive behaviours by the manager lead to an ongoing and heightened state of fear, as the targets/ observers anticipate and fear the leader's threats to their career, work life and wellbeing. When the targets don't feel they can cope with the situation, fear leads them to engage in self-protective and avoidant behaviours (Kiewitz, Restubog, Shoss, Garcia & Tang, 2016).

Anger

A negative event that an individual holds another responsible for will engender an emotion of anger. Therefore, targets are likely to feel angry when they perceive that actions by their manager will block their personal goals, such as job security, performance achievement, professional reputation or growth and development. When abuse is directed towards several team members, individuals making sense of why they are experiencing sustained abuse are more likely to focus sole responsibility on the leader and to believe that the mistreatment is not deserved. Therefore, they feel anger when humiliated by the leader or when the leader fails to meet their expectations of how they feel they should be treated. The more targets believe they are not responsible for the abuse, the more intense their anger is likely to be. Intense anger may then predispose targets to perceive, interpret and act on future events from a more hostile perspective and as a result become predisposed to experiencing anger, even with quite minor triggers (Peng et al., 2019; Tepper, 2007).

Shame

While a negative event that an individual holds another responsible for will engender an emotion of anger, a negative event that an individual holds *themselves* responsible for will produce shame. Shame arises when an individual's self-concept is threatened – that is, their self-worth, personal identity or social identity. This feeling of shame occurs when targets appraise themselves as accountable for the abusive behaviour they are receiving from their manager. Abusive leaders often blame targets for their inadequacies or attack them interpersonally. As a result, targets may blame themselves for incurring mistreatment due to their own inadequacies or lack of social skills, reducing their feelings of self-worth and arousing feelings of shame. Employees may also feel they should speak up about the abuse and, when they don't, they feel shame at their avoidance of the issue. Feelings of shame are also likely to be stronger when co-workers report being subjected to lower levels of abuse compared to the target (Peng et al., 2019; Plate, 2015; Webster et al., 2016).

In some cases, targets may hold both themselves and the abusive leader responsible – that is, when co-workers also report experiencing abuse. They may try to recover and protect their self-image by engaging in impression management activities, to create a positive image of being a good and dedicated employee (e.g., coming to work early, working harder, working long hours or weekends). Targets and observers are most likely to exhibit these sorts of behaviours when they feel the stress of the situation can be reduced by their actions (Kim, Holtz & Hu, 2020; Peng et al., 2019). If targets fail to understand why they are feeling powerless, trapped, isolated and undermined by their manager, they are likely to become self-critical as a result of feeling shame, which can result in avoidant and submissive behaviours (Fatima, Majeed & Jahanzeb, 2020). If they are unable to develop shame resilience (e.g., understanding what is causing the shame) and they feel forced to stay in an abusive environment over time, they may experience emotional exhaustion.

Emotional exhaustion and burnout

When targets experience sustained stress over time, as a result of mistreatment and difficult interpersonal interactions with their manager, the resulting emotional exhaustion (e.g., mental fatigue and lack of energy) depletes their resources, leading to serious levels of psychological distress. Targets must expend a lot of psychological and emotional resources in their effort to handle this interpersonal stressor. Emotional exhaustion results when the emotional demands of dealing with an abusive manager exceed the individual's resources to cope with the situation (Breevaart, Bakker, Hetland & Hetland, 2014; Chi & Liang, 2013; Wu & Hu, 2009). The level of emotional exhaustion experienced may be moderated by the use of ingratiation tactics (e.g., flattery or performing favours for the leader), which may restore feelings of autonomy (Harvey, Stoner, Hochwarter & Kacmar, 2007).

Destructive leadership behaviours persisting over time result in follower burnout, specifically emotional exhaustion, cynicism and depersonalisation (a persistent feeling of observing oneself from outside one's body, the sense that the situation isn't real and increased mental distance from the job; Breevaart et al., 2014; Schaufeli, Leiter & Maslach, 2009). Even passive leadership styles can lead to burnout through the lack of clear expectations, roles and responsibilities and the resulting work overload (Vullinghs, De Hoogh, Den Hartog & Boon, 2020). Another contributor to burnout is a conflict between personal values, the espoused values of the organisation and values in action, as demonstrated by the destructive actions of the leader. Burnout leads to reduced job performance, job satisfaction and organisational commitment and more serious health problems, all resulting in increased sickness absenteeism.

EMPLOYEE BEHAVIOURAL RESPONSES TO DESTRUCTIVE LEADERSHIP

Employees may respond to destructive leadership in a range of ways. Initially, they may try to solve the problem they are facing or influence the leader to improve their behaviour. Due to the risk of retaliatory responses by the leader to their influencing efforts, a target may seek to reduce their supervisor's abuse by engaging in positive behaviours such as working harder (Mitchell & Ambrose, 2012). If these efforts do not bring results, they are likely to withdraw from the work environment (tardiness, absenteeism and turnover; Tepper et al., 2017). Often, destructive leadership results in employee reactions that are destructive and costly for organisations, such as non-compliance, deviance or theft (Tepper, Duffy, Henle & Lambert, 2006).

Retaliation, interpersonal deviance and organisational deviance

There is considerable evidence of the relationship between abusive supervision and supervisor-directed hostility and aggression. The extent to which targets retaliate can be moderated by the individual's motivation and ability to control their actions and the extent to which the leader has power to withhold rewards or to punish them for retaliating by escalating their abusive behaviours (Lian et al., 2014; Mitchell & Ambrose, 2012). Anger leads to interpersonal aggression against the leader responsible, and over time, these hostile feelings may generalise to displaying deviant behaviour against co-workers. For example, when aggressing against the offending leader is not a viable option, targets may displace their aggression by venting their frustration on co-workers. Angry individuals may speak in loud and impatient tones and display hostile body language, such as frowning. As a result, co-workers may withdraw from their angry presence, confirming the individual's negative interpretation of the situation and fuelling further interpersonal deviance (Peng et al., 2019). There is also evidence that interpersonal aggression that is triggered by abusive supervision may intensify in targets who intend to leave the organisation (Richard, Boncoeur, Chen & Ford, 2020; Tepper et al., 2009).

Negative emotions resulting from experiencing destructive leadership are related to increased deviant behaviour at work (e.g., taking long breaks, stealing and/or sabotage), including interpersonal deviance (e.g., gossiping, aggression and verbal abuse). Such negative emotions increase the target's levels of scepticism, so they are more likely to detect deviance in others that they can use to justify engaging in organisational deviance themselves. As they become more cynical, they are more likely to act in deviant ways because they view their manager as dishonest or abusive (Gkorezis, Petridou & Krouklidou,

2015; Michel, Newness & Duniewicz, 2016). High power-distance employees (where hierarchical authority is valued) are more likely to experience guilt and shame when experiencing abusive supervision, driving them to act more deviantly. Targets are also more likely to engage in organisational deviance when they perceive their co-workers are approving of it or their co-workers themselves are engaging in organisational deviance (Chintakananda & Greguras, 2017; Tepper, Henle, Lambert, Giacalone & Duffy, 2008).

Presenteeism, absenteeism and turnover

Due to the pressure being applied by their managers and the consequential stress and job insecurity, targets often continue to come to work in spite of the health problems they may be experiencing. This results in presenteeism, where employees are physically present but mentally absent, reducing their productivity and increasing the potential of making mistakes. Such workers will go through the motions of work while their attention is directed elsewhere (Gilbreath & Karimi, 2012; Molino, Cortese & Ghislieri, 2019). If the target is trying to avoid negative feedback and abuse from their manager through working harder, they may exhibit workaholism as a dysfunctional coping strategy, and workaholism is associated with presenteeism and sickness absence. There is some evidence that employees' anxiety and depression levels may mediate between destructive leadership and employee behaviours such as poor job performance and intention to quit (Mathur & Chauhan, 2018; Pyc, Meltzer & Liu, 2017).

Ultimately, employees are likely to cope with experiencing strong negative emotions (e.g., fear, shame, disappointment and frustration) over a significant period of time by withdrawing. Reduced job satisfaction leads to increased absenteeism and intentions to quit (Akca, 2017; Kim et al., 2020; Labrague, Nwafor & Tsaras, 2020; Mathieu & Babiak, 2016). This effect is likely to be heightened when abuse is also directed towards work colleagues (Peng et al., 2019).

ROLE OF EMPLOYEES IN DESTRUCTIVE LEADERSHIP

Employees impacted by destructive leadership are likely to display a range of reactions, depending on both their personal characteristics and the resources and level of support they can access. Their responses are likely to have consequences for the way the leader interacts with them (Milosevic, Maric & Lončar, 2020). Hernandez and Sitkin (2012) proposed that followers can try to influence leaders to behave more ethically by engaging in ethical decisions and actions or influencing their leader to forgo unethical actions. For example, such followers can become a whistle-blower (high risk) or a trusted advisor to the leader through a demonstration of concern and support. The leader's response is likely to depend on whether they see the follower's behaviour as strengthening the relationship through helpful or co-operative behaviours, or damaging the relationship through challenging their behaviour. Followers can draw on the leader's personal values, priorities and responsibilities to direct their attention to behaviours that may not be ethical. Alternatively, they could pose a provocative comparison to someone the leader does not want to be compared to, in an effort to influence the leader to choose not to engage in unethical behaviours.

In the context of destructive leadership, May, Wesche, Heinitz and Kerschreiter (2014) discussed how the level of confrontation displayed by the follower towards their destructive leader influenced the leader's own perceptions of the follower – that is, the degree to which the leader perceived their follower to be aggressive, retaliatory, constructive or submissive. They suggested the level of follower confrontation would influence how leaders perceived the follower to be dealing with their leadership and would determine their behaviour in response to the follower. May et al. (2014) proposed that perceptions by leaders of the followers' coping responses (e.g., submissive and/or aggressive reactions from followers) would result in leaders engaging in further destructive leadership behaviour. If they perceived the coping response as constructive, they would limit their abusive behaviour towards the individual. While this synthesis is useful, there are three key limitations with this approach: (a) the leader must be able to observe the follower's coping strategy to be able to perceive it as submissive, aggressive or constructive, and emotion-focused strategies in particular are largely unobservable; (b) the leader's perception of the follower's coping behaviour may not be accurate; and (c) the leader must have the resources and inclination to follow up with constructive behaviour when responding to follower responses to their behaviour.

ROLE OF CO-WORKERS AND THIRD-PARTY OBSERVERS IN DESTRUCTIVE LEADERSHIP

As discussed above, the behaviour of co-workers can strongly influence the behaviour of targets of abuse, by, for example, encouraging mistreated employees to engage in workplace deviance. Research has explored how third-party observers and co-workers react to injustice and undeserving mistreatment of colleagues by the manager and when colleagues are more inclined to engage in prosocial behaviour towards targets. The quality of the relationship between the third party and the target will impact the level to which protective action will be taken by the third party to help alleviate their suffering. When observers experience survivor guilt (an accidental advantage over their colleague), they attempt to alleviate such guilt by providing assistance and support to the target. Witnessing abuse by a manager towards a target can lead to bystanders experiencing vicarious abusive supervision, which can produce supervisor-directed deviance and support for the targeted employee. However, if third parties consider the target deserving of the mistreatment, they may be more motivated to exclude the targeted co-worker (Chen & Liu, 2019; Mitchell, Vogel & Folger, 2015; Priesemuth, 2013; Priesemuth & Schminke, 2019).

Human resources (HR) employees are also affected. They have been posited as the 'toxin handlers' who deal with toxic emotions at work, arising from issues such as abusive behaviours from managers, in an effort to sustain a humane and respectful work culture (Daniel, 2017). HR employees are tasked with dealing with the dire consequences of destructive leadership for organisations, including, for example, reduced employee engagement, work engagement and productivity and increased presenteeism, absenteeism and turnover. The very mechanisms put in place to protect employees can become instruments of harm in the context of destructive leadership. For example, formal investigations of complaints or bullying reports undertaken by HR officers are kept confidential, to protect employees' privacy. Consequently, investigations can easily become long and drawn out, where no parties can be regularly updated or informed of what is happening, thereby irreparably damaging working relationships. HR personnel are charged with the duty of helping employees reduce their emotional pain, while being aware of the need to maximise productivity and keep the organisation profitable. Working behind closed doors, their work is virtually invisible. They are often unable to reduce the anxiety and fear being experienced by workers, and they may even contribute to workers' anxiety and stress by implementing official policies and processes that produce more distress. HR professionals are in the invidious position of being expected to provide a solution when they are part of the organisational system. Having to handle high-tension, emotional situations, often with little support or respite, makes them particularly susceptible to emotional exhaustion and burnout. HR professionals can risk their own careers by speaking up or initiating formal action against an offending senior manager. Organisational development (OD) teams who are called in after the fact have the challenge of assisting the team to resolve internal conflicts (e.g., between workers who spoke up and those who remained silent), repair damaged relationships and rebuild team functioning (Daniel, 2017, 2020).

PRACTICAL IMPLICATIONS

The challenge for organisational representatives, such as HR officers, and for external consultants/coaches is how best to guide employees to make informed choices about how to react to abuse and mistreatment from their manager, in ways that are most suitable for their wellbeing and career. In addition to ensuring employees are aware of the relevant policies and procedures to support them, employees may be offered training in stress management, as well as provided with access to mediation and counselling services, all of which can be initiated by HR officers.

CONCLUSION

Destructive leadership causes psychological, emotional, physical and career harm to employees at work, and displaced negative emotions and conflict can extend to their families. In this chapter, we have acknowledged that employees are just as likely to display ineffective reactions (e.g., feeling fear, anger and shame or lodging a formal complaint) as they are to engage in effective responses. Employees dealing with abuse from their manager typically move from a problem-solving focus, such as challenging the leader, to emotion-focused coping, specifically avoidance. Avoidance strategies can be effective over short periods of time (to recover energy and regroup) but are less effective in the long term and may actually cause the abuse to escalate. Resiliency and coping theories are useful in informing our understanding of how employees maintain wellbeing and build their resilience to the dire consequences of destructive leadership. These are discussed in more detail in Chapter 8.

FOLLOWER COPING WITH DESTRUCTIVE LEADERSHIP

CHAPTER OVERVIEW

This chapter discusses how followers commonly cope with experiences of destructive leadership. The key coping frameworks are described, and both effective and ineffective coping strategies are identified. Effective coping strategies primarily focus on directly reducing or resolving the problem and, in the case of destructive leadership, commonly include confronting the leader with the impact of their behaviour, seeking assistance from senior managers or from sources external to the organisation and removing oneself from the situation via an internal transfer or via external employment. Ineffective coping strategies focus on an individual's response to the issue (rather than the issue itself) and include, for example, worrying, feeling shame and confusion and avoidance of the situation (i.e., work absenteeism). We also discuss the value of seeking and receiving social support as a coping strategy when experiencing destructive leadership.

COPING WITH DESTRUCTIVE LEADERSHIP

The preceding chapter (Chapter 7) discussed the consequences of destructive leadership experiences for the follower, including mental health issues, withdrawal, reduced work performance and ultimately employee turnover. This chapter focuses on the common coping responses employed by followers to cope with (i.e., manage) workplace destructive leadership. Experiencing destructive leadership is a significant source of occupational stress. If the destructive leadership experiences are prolonged, then *chronic* stress reactions are highly likely to occur, impacting the follower, other colleagues, the follower's health and their personal relationships. Experiences of workplace conflict commonly include interpersonal conflicts, bullying, harassment and destructive leadership, although of course destructive leadership may include *all* these forms of conflict. Unfortunately, workplace conflict is an increasing problem and accounts for a significant proportion of formal workplace mental health injury (e.g., stress) claims and their costs (Webster, Brough & Daly, 2016).

Accepted explanations of stress describe it as a continual process between an individual and their environment. When the environment becomes too demanding or dangerous, individuals perceive and cognitively process this danger (via a process of cognitive appraisal) and consider their options to reduce or manage this danger – that is, to cope with it (Brough, Drummond & Biggs, 2018). Thus, it is the identification or perception of stress that elicits a coping reaction: 'when the individual discovers some important motive or value is being threatened, coping activity is mobilized by virtue of this threat, by virtue of the cognition that: "My life, health, wealth, or cherished social relationships are in danger"' (Lazarus, 1966, p. 153). This process of stress identification involves two key cognitive components. *Primary appraisal* is first triggered in response to exposure to a stressful event and involves an assessment by the individual as to whether the event poses a potential threat to their wellbeing, and the degree of that threat. If the event is appraised as a threat, *secondary appraisal* occurs to determine the individual's perceived ability to cope with and manage the threat, including an evaluation of their available resources, such as potential courses of action they might be able to take. Such cognitive appraisals determine whether the individual views the stressor as a challenge that they feel able to confront with some level of confidence and that may enhance their wellbeing. Alternatively, as is likely in the case of destructive leadership, the stressor can be perceived to be a threat to their psychological, emotional or physical health and wellbeing (Raper & Brough, 2021).

If coping is successful, the environmental danger or stimuli cease. If the stimuli continue, other forms of coping can be tried. The physical and mental health impacts of chronic stress occur when an individual cannot reduce the toxic environmental stimuli. Instead, the individual is placed under constant pressure and a persistent state of alertness. In this situation, a range of coping behaviours can be adopted, including ones that provide a short-term 'escape' for the individual from the situation, including, for example, work withdrawal and absenteeism and increased intake of alcohol, drugs and food (Bamberger & Bacharach, 2006; O'Driscoll, Brough & Kalliath, 2009). These forms of coping are classified as '*emotion-focused*' coping behaviours. Other more direct forms of coping are focused on actively reducing the environmental stimuli, such as seeking advice and changing the situation in some way, and these are labelled *'problem-focused'* coping strategies. It is important to note that these coping behaviours are not mutually exclusive. Instead, in a highly stressful situation, most people adopt both types of coping behaviours. Figure 8.1 illustrates this dual classification of coping and their associated coping behaviours.

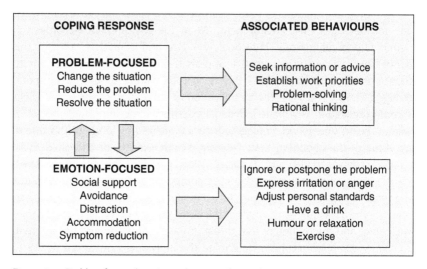

Figure 8.1 Problem-focused coping and emotion-focused coping.

It is also important to consider the interplay between the physical and psychological stress and coping processes commonly produced when experiencing destructive leadership. A stress and coping model by Selye (1956, 1976) is especially pertinent. Selye (1956) described how individuals progress through three stages in response to chronic stress experiences:

1. **Alarm.** The alarm stage is the body's initial response to a stressor and is characterised by a decline in normal functioning. Common physiological symptoms include hormone secretions, gastrointestinal ulcers, loss of body weight, weakened immune system and inflammation. We can also include behavioural symptoms here, such as change in sleep patterns (e.g., more disturbed sleep) and changes in an individual's normal self-care habits, such as undertaking less exercise, eating more junk food, drinking more alcohol, etc. Psychological symptoms primarily include increased anxiety, irritability, worry, ruminating about interactions with the

leader and low mood or depression. This stage is also where workplace-avoidance behaviours will occur, such as increased numbers of days off on sick leave, missing meetings and withdrawal from the normal workplace social activities.

2. **Adaptation.** The adaptation stage occurs over time (i.e., *chronic* stress experiences) and concerns the body's ability to resist or adapt to the continuing stressor. Thus, a worker's hopes that the destructive leadership experiences will stop or change have not materialised, and instead the worker adapts to the ongoing stress. Psychologically, adaptation is a learning process. Thus, we 'adapt' to the destructive leadership behaviours, by trying to understand these behaviours and prevent their occurrence, for example, by physically avoiding the leader, avoiding being alone with them or avoiding 'provoking' them. Adaptation is also where proactive (problem-focused) coping behaviours are engaged, as we discussed above, such as seeking help and support, considering practical options (e.g., transferring to a different team/department) and attempts to reduce the stressor by discussing it with the leader in question, other managers, colleagues and/or human resources. In the face of this chronic stressor, which workers may feel powerless to change, emotion-focused coping behaviours can also occur that do not address the leader's behaviours directly but instead focus on making the worker feel better (or numb) in the short term, including excessive alcohol or drug intake.

3. **Exhaustion**. The exhaustion stage occurs when further adaptation to the chronic stressor can no longer occur. Typically, we identify severe strain, burnout or breakdowns with this final stage, presenting as either mental or physical health manifestations such as heart attacks, organ failure, chronic fatigue, mental breakdowns and suicidal thoughts or attempts. It is important to recognise that this final exhaustion stage is not necessarily permanent or fatal. If the stressor ceases, then, after a period of rest and recovery, health can be restored. The extent of the individual's recovery to pre-stress levels does, of course, vary considerably. This is largely based on the degree and extent of stress experienced and the availability of resources to assist the worker in the adaption or recovery stages. Returning a worker to the same stressful work conditions after a period of sick leave, for example, is obviously not conducive to their long-term recovery.

Some research has specifically focused on how workers commonly cope with destructive leadership experiences. Yagil, Ben-Zur and Tamir (2011) described the development of a Coping with Abusive Supervision Scale, assessing five coping responses: *ingratiation, direct communication, avoidance of contact, support-seeking* and *reframing*. Yagil et al. reported that participants employed all five coping responses, although as the destructive leadership experiences escalated, participants reported an increased use of avoidance coping strategies to gain emotional relief from the abuse. Yagil et al. concluded that most individual employees don't know how to cope effectively with abusive supervision.

Skinner, Edge, Altman and Sherwood (2003) proposed a framework of 12 coping strategies as specific responses to stress: *problem solving, information seeking, opposition, negotiating, self-reliance, seeking support, delegation, accommodation/distracting, submission, helplessness, escape* and *isolation/withdrawal*. Again, it can be seen that these coping strategies include both problem-focused and emotion-focused behaviours, as we described above. In another assessment of how followers cope with destructive leadership, May, Wesche, Heinitz and Kerschreiter (2014) reported that these workers engaged in multiple problem-focused and emotion-focused coping strategies varying in the level to which they confronted the leader (e.g., degree of assertiveness and aggressiveness of the coping behaviour). Problem-focused coping included strategies such as challenging the leader's behaviour, employing upward influencing tactics, such as ingratiation, or seeking instrumental support. Emotion-focused coping included strategies such as cognitive restructuring (reframing) and seeking emotional support. May et al. (2014) also included functional coping responses, such as ingratiation and negotiating better treatment from the leader, as well as dysfunctional coping responses, such as retaliation by verbally attacking or ridiculing the supervisor and/or their co-workers.

Webster et al. (2016) drew on both Yagil et al.'s (2011) coping responses and Skinner et al.'s (2003) framework to describe 12 families of coping behaviours to categorise followers' coping responses to destructive leadership. They identified 14 frequently utilised coping strategies by the respondents, which included problem-focused coping strategies such as *instrumental action*, exemplified by making a formal complaint, seeking mediation, bypassing their leader and speaking out about the issue (e.g., to senior managers). The respondents reported that these coping strategies were the most helpful in bringing about a resolution to the problem. The most frequently reported emotion-focused strategies included: *accommodation* (e.g., working harder), *submission* (e.g., rumination), *helplessness* and *delegation* (e.g., feeling shame; see Table 8.1). These coping strategies are clearly not proactive and are focused on aiding the respondents to feel better in a situation where they feel powerless to prevent the abuse from reoccurring.

Webster et al. (2016) also found that the most frequently reported ways of coping when dealing with toxic leadership were *seeking social support, leaving the organisation or taking leave, ruminating* and *challenging the leader*. Other reported coping strategies included problem-solving strategies, such as instrumental action (e.g., making a formal complaint, seeking mediation, whistleblowing) and information seeking (e.g., seeking professional advice), and emotion-focused strategies, such as self-reliance (e.g., working harder) or helplessness and delegation (e.g., feelings of shame, self-blame and disgust). Although some of these emotion-focused coping responses can be considered maladaptive, research indicates that these are common strategies employed when an individual feels powerless to prevent ongoing abuse and that, as we noted above, avoidance coping can be useful over the short-term, primarily by enabling workers to escape the situation momentarily (Nandkeolyar, Shaffer, Li, Ekkirala & Bagger, 2014).

Table 8.1   Examples of follower coping strategies after exposure to destructive leadership.

Coping strategies	Coping examples
Assertively confronting or challenging leader	*'I used problem-solving behaviours. I confronted the bullies'.* *'I stood my ground and defended myself when confronted'.* *'My approach was to have straight talks with the manager'.*
Direct communication	*'At first I attempted to clarify expectations and roles'.* *'I initially tried to coach my manager when certain behaviours started to impact on the team'.*
Instrumental action	*'We attempted whistle blowing but it went nowhere through official channels. The only option was to leave'.* *'I chose to document each incident and make sure it was witnessed'.* *'I made numerous attempts to discuss issues as they arose... I finally attempted a formal mediation process that failed completely....'* *'I openly challenged and raised the issues as a grievance through a formal process and resigned'.*
Undertaking health and wellbeing activities	*'I undertook activities such as yoga, breathing exercises, and increased my walking activities'.* *'I exercised by running every day, and I think this helped with the stress'.* *'I exercise every day, and try to eat healthy, because it keeps me feeling relaxed and fit during the day'.*
Social support: colleagues	*'I found one other colleague with whom I could debrief and that made things more bearable'.* *'I had a small network of people I had worked with previously with whom I was able to vent'.*

(Continued)

Table 8.1   (Continued)

Coping strategies	Coping examples
Social support: family and friends	*'Support from other senior leaders in the company who had left'.* *'Spent a lot of time discussing the situation with my husband and other friends'.* *'I coped by being supported by friends and family'.*
Leaving the situation	*'Ultimately it led to my taking 3 months stress leave'.* *'I took some sick leave when it got too much'.* *'...on advice from the Human Resources (HR) Manager and my Dr I removed myself from the environment and have been on my accrued sick and recreational leave since'.*
Bypassing the leader	*'The section in which I worked tended to work around the person, forming our own informal work groups to solve problems and make the work happen'.* *'I chose to not engage with the manager'.* *'I just managed to get through each day with little or no personal contact with him'.*
Ignoring the leader	*'Low profile - don't question or challenge'.* *'I would ignore and not respond to the behaviour so I believe my strategies were submissive, rather than assertive'.*
Cognitive restructuring	*'I have focused on what I can get out of a bad employment situation'.* *'I had to work hard to maintain a sense of inner calm and manage my state of mind'.*
Seeking professional support and advice	*'Saw my GP to have the incident and my reaction documented in case there are further incidents which may make me consider stress leave'.* *'I contacted the HR group manager for advice'.*
Rumination	*'I still feel disgust and outraged that basic human rights, like the right to feel safe, to feel protected from bullying and harassment, is not even represented in some of the institutions that purport to study it'.* *'I had lost a sense of proportion or perspective because of how odd and surreal everything was'.*
Working harder	*'Worked really hard, lots of extra hours, compliant'.* *'I came in put my head down and worked'.*
Feelings of helplessness	*'Had a sense of helplessness around the options'.* *'Do I still doubt and feel insecure about my ability to do my work - totally - there is nothing I do not question or analyse to death'.*
Shame	*'I actually feel sick when I look back on it. It was so shameful that a group of intelligent, thoughtful articulate staff were completely unable to meet the challenge of addressing this director's behaviour'.* *'I still feel degraded and annoyed at myself for allowing that behaviour to be conducted towards me'.*

Source: Adapted from Webster, Brough and Daly (2016, Table 2).

Webster et al. (2016) also reported that many respondents who had experienced toxic supervision took extended sick leave or left the organisation once their preferred coping strategies had failed and the destructive leader behaviours continued. Employees who remained in the workplace reported a variety of adverse consequences. Promotion of organisational policies and procedures, codes of conduct, employee assistance programmes and other external counselling services are basic requirements to promote employee wellbeing; however, they are often inadequate to deal effectively with this specific problem. Instead, Webster et al. (2016) recommended that proactive organisational training programmes focusing on effective coping strategies to deal with toxic behaviours, advice on the social and professional support available and an emphasis on the importance of taking responsibility for maintaining personal health and wellbeing assist in equipping employees with the knowledge and skills needed to prevent them from coming to harm, or to deflect harm when it first occurs.

It has also been noted that reacting to destructive leadership with passive coping strategies such as avoiding the leader, maintaining distance, avoiding communication and withholding organisationally relevant information from the leader has a direct destructive impact on both employees and on the broader organisational performance (Bhandarker & Rai, 2019). Thus, accommodating adverse supervision perpetuates a toxic work environment, which is detrimental for both the employee and for the organisation. It has also been suggested that experiencing destructive leadership can cause paranoia in employees as a consequential coping method of this toxic supervision. Thus, previous adverse supervision experiences can be carried over to a new role where employees anticipate adverse behaviours from their new supervisor (Lopes, Kamau & Jaspal, 2019). This lack of trust and increased suspicion of a new supervisor obviously works as a defence mechanism for the employee and is certainly an issue that should be identified and resolved by both the employee and the new supervisor.

THE ROLE OF SOCIAL SUPPORT

There has been considerable research on the role of social support in mitigating the negative impact of stressors. In fact, the degree of available support provides a direct buffer to protect individuals from their experienced stress. That is, support directly reduces the impact of the stress experienced (Brough et al., 2018).

This is why many occupational stress interventions, including programmes designed to reduce or prevent destructive leadership, contain strategies for employees to maximise their experiences of social support and/or aim to teach leaders how to be a more supportive supervisor (primarily in recognition that some destructive behaviours occur due to a leader's insecurity about their capabilities; Biggs, Brough & Barbour, 2014b; Gonzalez-Morales, Kernan, Becker & Eisenberger, 2018). As an interpersonal stressor, destructive leadership commonly threatens the follower's degree of received social support, potentially reducing this external resource and protection for employees. Strategies for gaining social support in the workplace, such as from effective ingratiation tactics, may increase the individual's perceived control, and this feeling of control (e.g., the perceived ability to cope with stressors) has been argued to improve individuals' coping abilities (Brough et al., 2018; Harvey, Stoner, Hochwarter & Kacmar, 2007).

Research has established that both the *sources* of social support (i.e., from managers, colleagues, family, friends) and the *types* of support (i.e., practical, emotional) received *and* provided are important for effective employee wellbeing, retention and job performance (Brough & Pears, 2004). However, support received from direct supervisors typically aids in reducing generic work stress (i.e., not stress *caused* by the supervisor) to a greater extent, as compared to colleague support. This is because supervisors commonly provide more instrumentation support, including provision of specific guidance and resources, to actively reduce the work stressor – for example, extra personnel or time to complete work tasks and to better manage workloads (Biggs, Brough & Barbour, 2014a; Brough & Pears, 2004). It has been reported that when coping specifically with destructive leadership, social support offered by colleagues may even *exacerbate* the negative impacts of these experiences. Social support from colleagues may encourage the individual to ruminate on and 're-live' the negative aspects of their experience, thus enhancing perceptions of stress and strain (Brough & Biggs, 2010; Wu & Hu, 2009). This especially applies to employees who are particularly susceptible to emotional contagion and are easily influenced by the emotions of others (Brough & Westman, 2018). Indeed, the transfer of both positive and negative emotions between work colleagues (including supervisors) is a topic of considerable research interest. Thus, the emotional consequences of adverse work incidents experienced by a colleague (e.g., toxic supervision) can be directly transferred to colleagues, significantly increasing their own respective levels of stress and strain and negatively impacting their job performance and work engagement (Brough, Westman, Chen & Chan, in press).

There is also evidence suggesting that negative interactions between colleagues (e.g., causing feelings of resentment or shame, making critical remarks, failing to provide the promised help, social undermining) negate the benefits of any received social support on the follower's psychological wellbeing and instead serve to aggravate their discomfort (Lincoln, 2000). This is primarily because co-workers themselves are also likely to be engaging in self-protective behaviours against the shared abuse of a common manager. This 'shared stressor' and the motivation to avoid being the target of a toxic supervisor can result in a *lack* of positive support for suffering colleagues. Indeed, many employees report lowered levels of friendliness and communication from their team members when dealing with toxic leadership, and instead their isolation and ostracism can increase (Webster et al., 2016).

Other research has reported a reduction in perceived abusive supervision when colleague support was high (Hobman, Restubog, Bordia & Tang, 2009). Peer support can provide a buffering effect in the face of a common enemy, the abusive manager. Seeking social support in order to discuss experiences with sympathetic colleagues, or to express anger or frustration, may provide the emotional support necessary to cope with the abuse and adverse work conditions created by their manager (Brough, 2005; Van Emmerik, Euwema & Bakker, 2007). It is also the case that support offered by family and friends directly reduces stress experiences in the work domain, even though this type of support is primarily emotional or instrumental (Brough, Hassan & O'Driscoll, 2014; Duffy, Ganster & Pagon, 2002).

When their assistance is sought, organisational representatives have a significant role in advising and supporting victims of destructive leadership behaviours. Many targets of destructive leadership report being as distressed by the lack of support received from their organisation as they are by the destructive behaviour to which they were subjected (see e.g., Brough, Lawrence, Tsahuridu & Brown, in press; Webster et al., 2016). When formal misconduct investigations are conducted in a workplace where employees do not feel in control of the situation and/or do not feel supported by the organisation, they may not actively participate in the investigation, and indeed this formal investigation can also be a cause of significant stress for the employee (Brough et al., in press). Instead of seeking advice and support from HR or employee assistance programmes, many employees report seeking social support from sources external to the organisation or, indeed, may exit the organisation entirely (Webster & Brough, 2015). Consequently, the true extent of leader misbehaviour and its impact upon employees is difficult to accurately assess.

Follower resiliency

Given the dire consequences of toxic leadership on followers, a consideration of follower resiliency is pertinent (Milosevic, Maric & Lončar, 2020; Winn & Dykes, 2019). The study of *resiliency* in the workplace is a relatively new area of research. Resiliency goes beyond the definition of resilience, which has been described as the capacity to rebound or bounce back from adversity, conflict or failure. Resiliency is the process by which wellbeing is restored and includes the characteristics that influence the return to a state of wellbeing following an adverse event (McLarnon & Rothstein, 2013). Resiliency incorporates what a person learns when dealing with adversity and the processes that lead to personal choices, career recovery and personal growth. Specifically, resiliency has been conceptualised as '*involving affective, cognitive, and behavioural self-regulatory processes to assist recovery and restoration of optimal functioning after a significant adverse workplace event or experience*' (McLarnon & Rothstein, 2013, p. 64). It is purported that the resiliency processes involve three domains: (a) self-regulation of beliefs or cognitions, (b) self-regulation of emotions and (c) engagement of behavioural strategies that provide a sense of personal control and personal self-efficacy. If successful, these adaptive responses will result in outcomes that demonstrate resilience has occurred (e.g., psychological, emotional and physical wellbeing). However, outcomes may differ depending on the situational context and the adversity experienced.

There is no conceptual model for resiliency in the context of destructive leadership, so we have adapted McLarnon and Rothstein's (2013) model of workplace resilience as a response to destructive leadership (see Figure 8.2). Followers exhibit an initial response to the traumatic work experience – in this instance, destructive leadership behaviours. Personal characteristics (e.g., follower type, self-efficacy, self-discipline) will affect the initial response (e.g., negative thoughts and emotions, perceived stress). The relationship between the target's initial response to perceiving destructive leadership behaviours, and the cognitive, emotional and behavioural self-regulatory processes they employ in response, will be mediated by their personal characteristics, as well as situational factors, such as supports and resources (e.g., social support from colleagues, friends and family, organisational support). Achieving positive life and work outcomes will depend on the effectiveness of their self-regulatory processes (e.g., their ability to understand and control ineffective thoughts and thinking patterns, negative emotions and counterproductive behaviours). In sum, the ability of an employee to return to a state of wellbeing is determined by their level of resiliency, and their coping skills will determine their resiliency in recovering from the experience of destructive leadership.

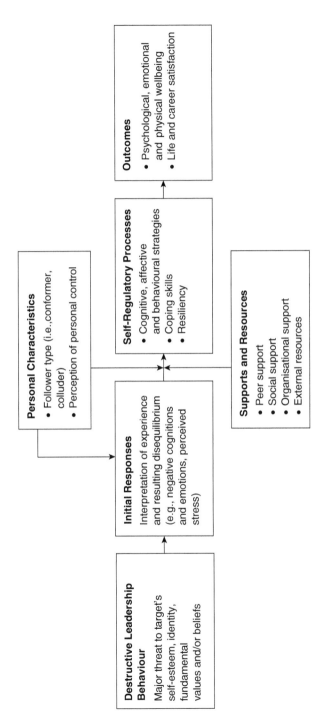

Figure 8.2 Conceptual model of follower resiliency to destructive leadership.

Source: Adapted from McLarnon and Rothstein (2013).

IMPLICATIONS FOR PRACTICE

Given the impact on followers of not responding effectively when experiencing destructive leadership, it is recommended organisations provide proactive training programmes that are focused on effective coping strategies to deal with toxic behaviours and that encourage employees to take personal responsibility for building their resiliency and maintaining their wellbeing.

CONCLUSION

Destructive leadership can certainly be perceived as an uncontrollable situation by an employee, and one where their coping efforts often have minimal impact on any positive change. When managing the stressful situation of destructive leadership, employees are just as likely to try ineffective coping strategies (e.g., worrying, feeling shame and confusion, avoidance) as they are to try more effective direct coping strategies aimed at actually resolving the problem. Emotion-focused coping strategies can be effective over short periods of time (i.e., to recover energy and regroup) but are usually less effective in the long term. Problem-focused coping responses aim to reduce or resolve the stressful situation in some way, and in the case of destructive leadership, these strategies commonly include seeking assistance from senior managers or from sources external to the organisation and removing oneself from the situation via an internal transfer or via external employment.

Further research is required to investigate functional versus dysfunctional coping strategies employed by followers to deal with the stressor of destructive leadership. Respondents may not report all the maladaptive coping mechanisms they employ, such as counterproductive work behaviours or problem drinking. Thus, the range of coping responses to destructive leadership proposed by Webster et al. (2016) would benefit from further validation. Similarly, further assessments of the benefits and hindrances of the use of social support as a coping strategy to successfully manage destructive leadership experiences are required.

SECTION 2

ORGANISATIONAL INTERVENTIONS TO ADDRESS DESTRUCTIVE LEADERSHIP

9

ORGANISATIONAL DIAGNOSTICS AND INTERVENTIONS

CHAPTER OVERVIEW

One of the commonly recommended strategies for protection against destructive leadership is to prevent its occurrence. This chapter provides a summary of the current assessment tools for diagnosing destructive leadership characteristics, with a review of the pros and cons for using these measures within organisational settings. We also discuss the diagnostics used to design workplace interventions in the context of destructive leadership and current trends in organisational interventions.

ORGANISATIONAL DIAGNOSTICS AND INTERVENTIONS

Organisational diagnostics, such as cultural and climate surveys, multisource feedback, high rates of complaints and grievances and patterns of leave or turnover in a particular department or team, can indicate the potential existence of destructive leadership that requires further investigation. Once identified, it is important organisations deal effectively with managers displaying destructive leadership behaviours, regardless of what power or status they hold. As discussed in previous chapters, organisations can foster destructive behaviour by focusing on achievement of strategic and operational goals at any cost, by only measuring outcomes and/or by punishing failures and non-achievement of key performance indicators. Where failure or underperformance is likely to result in punitive measures and/or non-achievement of incentives, the likelihood of activation of dark side traits and engagement in derailing behaviours increases. Organisations that focus on placing equal emphasis on how organisational goals are achieved – that is, the behaviours demonstrated in goal achievement, together with goal outcomes – are less likely to encourage destructive behaviours to ensure goal attainment (Bardes & Piccolo, 2010; Mawritz, Folger & Latham, 2014).

There are clear interventions to prevent organisations becoming conducive environments for destructive leadership practices. Such interventions include standard governance frameworks, codes of conduct, clearly articulated organisational values and policies, procedures and controls to detect and deal with leaders' destructive behaviour (Brough, Lawrence, Tsahuridu & Brown, in press; Tepper, 2007). Once destructive behaviour is detected, boards, executives and HR professionals have to decide how they will deal with the identified destructive leader. Lengthy investigations can make the situation worse. Destructive leaders often have good relationships with people in powerful positions, are politically and socially astute and are likely to become litigious when challenged; thus, removing them can be difficult, time consuming and costly. Careful planning, with expert legal advice, is often necessary. Therefore, including objective diagnostics as part of a prevention strategy is an effective option for organisations.

LEADER DIAGNOSTICS

A key prevention strategy is screening out leaders predisposed to engage in destructive leadership behaviours during selection processes for manager recruitment, leadership development programmes and succession management. While it is acknowledged this practice is more favourably viewed in Australia than in other countries (such as the USA), such testing provides an important mechanism to identify extreme levels of personality traits that may predispose leaders to derailment. Assessment results can flag potential obstacles to leadership effectiveness and allow further investigation of candidates, through behavioural simulations, behavioural interviewing and reference checks based on behavioural criteria, to prevent poor selection decisions. In addition, leadership profiles can be included as an onboarding tool, to plan strategies that address potential leader derailers before they are exhibited. Leader profiles can also be employed as a development tool, to assist leaders to identify their strengths and potential derailers, and to inform strategies that enhance their self-leadership.

Self-report leadership profiles

Two self-report measures of the characteristics of the dark side of leadership (leadership derailers and destructive leadership) are reviewed here, specifically selected as they are designed to be used within a normal population for selection and development purposes.

1. **Hogan Development Survey** (HDS) (Hogan & Hogan, 2001; PBC Hogan, 2020), distributed by Hogan Assessments, measures the dark side of personality, based on characteristics of clinical personality disorders outlined in the DSM-IV (American Psychiatric Association, 1994): *excitable, sceptical, cautious, reserved, leisurely, bold, mischievous, colourful, imaginative, diligent* and *dutiful*. Designed for use with normal populations, the HDS compares an individual's responses with a large HDS norm database to describe how the person's interpersonal style is perceived by others. Participants complete the HDS online, the assessment is untimed and the results reflect the level of risk that they will overdo their strengths and demonstrate dark side behaviours when fatigued, bored, stressed or uncertain. The HDS identifies behavioural tendencies that can help or hinder an individual's reputation and outlines how others will perceive their leadership, depending on whether they are at high, medium or low risk of defaulting to dark side characteristics (see Table 9.1).

Table 9.1   Hogan Development Survey (HDS) scales and risks.

Scale	Description of Risks
Excitable	This scale concerns working with passion and enthusiasm, but also being easily frustrated, moody, irritable and inclined to give up on projects and people. High scorers may display dramatic emotional peaks and valleys. Low scorers may appear to lack passion or urgency.
Sceptical	This scale concerns being alert for signs of deceptive behaviour in others and taking action when it is detected. High scorers may appear negative or cynical. Low scorers may be overly trusting and naïve.
Cautious	This scale concerns risk aversion, fear of failure and avoiding criticism. High scorers appear conservative and careful, but are reluctant to take risks, regardless of risk assessment. Low scorers may be willing to take risks without adequate risk assessment.
Reserved	This scale concerns seeming tough, aloof, remote and unconcerned with the feelings of others. High scorers may seem indifferent to the feelings of others. Low scorers may be too concerned about the feelings of others.
Leisurely	This scale concerns appearing to be friendly and co-operative, but actually following one's own agenda and quietly, but stubbornly, resisting others' agendas. High scorers may seem very agenda driven, and low scorers may appear to lack an agenda or direction.

(Continued)

Table 9.1   (Continued)

Scale	Description of Risks
Bold	This scale concerns seeming fearless, confident and self-assured, always expecting to succeed and unable to admit mistakes or learn from experience. High scorers may seem overly assertive, self-promoting and overly competitive. Low scorers appear to lack self-confidence and resolve.
Mischievous	This scale concerns seeming bright, impulsive, adventurous, risk-seeking and limit-testing. High scorers seem charming and interesting but may be at times devious and exploitative. Low scorers appear conservative, compliant and are likely to be unadventurous.
Colourful	This scale concerns seeming gregarious, fun, entertaining and enjoying being in the spotlight. High scorers appear fun and socially skilled but may be attention-seeking, dramatic and easily bored. Low scorers appear modest, unassuming, quiet and self-restrained.
Imaginative	This scale concerns seeming innovative, creative, possibly eccentric and sometimes self-absorbed. High scorers may seem impractical, unpredictable, self-absorbed and odd. Low scorers appear practical, rely on routine and often lack new ideas.
Diligent	This scale concerns being hardworking, detail-oriented and having high standards of performance for self and others. High scorers may be picky, overly conscientious and tend to micromanage. Low scorers may have poor attention to detail and tend to over-delegate.
Dutiful	This scale concerns being compliant, conforming and eager to please others. High scorers seem unassuming and may appear excessively eager to please superiors. Low scorers appear overly independent and seem to resent authority.

2. **TalentQ Dimensions** (TalentQ, 2013), distributed by Hay Group, is a personality profile that includes leadership derailers, also based on characteristics of clinical personality disorders outlined in the DSM-IV (American Psychiatric Association, 1994): *hyper-sensitivity*, *eccentricity*, *exhibitionism*, *over-dependence*, *isolation*, *iconoclasm*, *over-confidence* and *micromanagement*. Candidates are presented with statements about behaviour at work and they rate each one indicating how true it is, from 'completely untrue' to 'very true'. Fifteen dimensions are measured. Participants complete Dimensions online, the assessment is untimed and the results include a derailment report (see Table 9.2).

Table 9.2   TalentQ Dimensions: Derailment factors and risks.

Factor	Description of Risks
Hyper-sensitivity	High scorers tend to be emotionally fragile, to feel victimised or persecuted, may be easily frustrated and irritated and lack the resilience to cope with difficult problems. They may be preoccupied with hidden agendas and politics, are inclined to view others' intentions as hostile or misinterpret innocent remarks. They are anxious, fearful and overly sensitive to criticism. Low scorers may be overly trusting or may not be sensitive enough to handle politically charged situations.

Factor	Description of Risks
Isolation	High scorers tend to be less comfortable in team situations, preferring to work on their own. They may avoid the company of others, be unable to consult adequately or operate within a network. Low scorers may have too much need to have other people around them, may be too sensitive to the opinions of others and may be afraid to make tough decisions that could be unpopular.
Eccentricity	High scorers tend to be poor listeners, being too intent on finding their own novel solutions to problems. They tend to make up their own rules and fail to comply with normal conventions. Their ideas may not be workable in practice. Low scorers risk being too analytical or conservative in their approach. They may lack the courage to face up to challenges.
Iconoclasm	High scorers tend to be tough minded and are liable to go to excess in breaking with rules and accepted conventions. They can fail to take account of other people's opinions and warnings and may even engage in anti-social or unethical behaviours. Low scorers conform with society's rules, but may appear complacent, passive or overly tolerant of others, lacking a strong character of their own.
Exhibitionism	High scorers need to be in the limelight, commanding the attention of others. They crave speed, variety and success in all aspects of their lives. They may make mistakes through being overly optimistic or unwilling to see the 'downside'. Low scorers tend to lack social confidence and charisma, can tend towards pessimism and may not respond well to new challenges.
Over-confidence	High scorers tend towards arrogance, lack a sense of their own limitations and can easily over-reach themselves. They may develop grandiose but unworkable visions that do not adequately deal with the underlying complexity of the problems involved. Their need to lead in any situation, to win and eclipse others will sometimes catch up with them. Low scorers may be troubled by feelings of under-confidence. Their modesty may inhibit them from trying to solve complex or strategic problems and they may not dare to be innovative. They may try to avoid competitive situations. They will prefer to follow rather than lead.
Over-dependence	High scorers avoid seeking to be a leader or influence others. Their need for careful reflection means they will not cope well with situations involving risk. Their desire to be agreeable may result in compliance and a lack of courage. Low scorers are more likely to depend on themselves, rely on their own judgement and may even resent attempts by others to lead, influence or dominate them. They may avoid consulting or taking advice from others. They are prone to making quick, risky decisions and their high level of stamina may get on other people's nerves.
Micromanagement	High scorers are over-reliant on structure, rules and detail. They may be inflexible, having difficulty adapting their behaviour to new circumstances or challenges. They may struggle to deal with unstructured situations or decisions for which there is inadequate data available. They tend to manage others too closely. Low scorers avoid bureaucracy, demonstrate a low level of reliability to fulfil their commitments, lack discipline and attention to detail and cannot be relied upon to keep to deadlines.

360-degree leader feedback

When considering candidates for promotion to a managerial role or in developmental settings, using a self-report measure alone to diagnose dark side characteristics of leadership has been criticised, due to the likelihood of target participants manipulating the tool or providing self-inflated ratings. A 360-degree feedback mechanism that includes self-report, manager, peer and direct report and other observations can be an effective way to capture the combination or pattern of effects of destructive leadership by assessing the disparity between self and raters' responses (Biggs, Brough & Barbour, 2014a; Gentry, Hannum, Ekelund & de Jong, 2007). However, conducting 360-degree feedback assessments on destructive managers who exhibit arrogant, intimidating and/or manipulative behaviour may result in raters choosing not to participate or choosing not to be truthful in their feedback, for fear of reprisals. Four 360-degree tools that purport to measure dark side leadership constructs are summarised here:

1. **Benchmarks®** (Centre for Creative Leadership) measures the concept of career derailers, with an assessment of problems that can stall a career in the second section of their tool: problems with interpersonal skills, difficulty building and leading a team, difficulty changing or adapting, failure to meet business objectives and being too narrow in functional orientation (assessing technical competency). The scales that relate directly to dark side traits fall under the section on *Difficulty building and leading a team*, where it specifically asks about arrogance, having a dictatorial approach, being emotionally volatile and adopting a bullying style under stress. In addition, there are some measures of manipulating and ego-centred behaviours under *Failure to meet business objectives* – for example, asking whether the participant overestimates his/her abilities, makes a splash then moves on without completing tasks or is self-promoting without results (Leslie & Velsor, 1996).

2. **Leadership Versatility Index (LVI)** assumes that leaders have situational strengths and asks respondents to rate whether the leader displays too little, the right amount or too much of four leadership styles, based on the versatile leadership model: *forceful leadership, enabling leadership, strategic leadership* and *operational leadership* (Kaiser, LeBreton & Hogan, 2015).

3. **CLS360** is based on a leadership circumplex made up of eight octants: inspirational, coaching, participative, yielding, directive, authoritarian, distrustful and withdrawn. The three octants associated with dark side

behaviours are *authoritarian* (i.e., harsh and reluctant to accept criticism), *distrustful* (i.e., distant from subordinates and suspicious of their motives) and *withdrawn* (i.e., avoiding confrontations and responsibilities) (Redeker, de Vries, Rouckhout, Vermeren & de Fruyt, 2014).

4. **Hogan 360** assesses the respondent's reputation, and how their behaviour is perceived by others. Feedback from managers, peers and direct reports highlights good and bad habits and makes it possible to target behaviours requiring improvement. When administering the Hogan personality assessments in conjunction with Hogan 360, it can identify if the predicted behaviour in the self-report measures is confirmed by observer ratings. Some managers exhibit a strong sense of self-awareness, as evidenced by learned positive behaviours, while others may have a difficult time overcoming dark side derailment issues (Hogan & Hogan, 2001).

RESEARCH MEASURES OF DESTRUCTIVE LEADERSHIP

When researching destructive leadership, a number of diagnostics are commonly included as assessments in larger research studies. For leader derailment or destructive leadership studies, for example, the Hogan HDS is often employed in research and is suitable for research in organisational settings. Other measures such as the assessment of psychopathy or dark triad characteristics are rarely used in organisational settings and are more commonly employed with student samples in research methodologies. Common research measures of destructive leadership that have been tested in normal populations include the following:

- *Abusive Supervision*, a 12-item measure of perceptions of abusive supervision (Tepper, 2000) and a shortened five-item measure (Mitchell & Ambrose, 2007).
- *Destructive Leadership Questionnaire* (DLQ), measuring perceptions of the current leader, regardless of whether the leader is a good, destructive or average leader, rating the extent to which the leader has characteristics or engages in behaviours associated with destructive leadership (Shaw, Erickson & Harvey, 2011).
- *Narcissistic Personality Inventory* (NPI), a 16-item version, measuring grandiose narcissism (Ames, Rose & Anderson, 2006).
- *Mach IV*, measuring four factors of Machiavellianism: distrust of others, desire for status, desire for control and amoral manipulation (Christie & Geis, 1970).

- *Machiavellian Personality Scale* (MPS), a 16-item measure of Machiavellianism, derived from the Mach IV (Dahling, Whitaker & Levy, 2009).
- *The Psychopathic Personality Inventory* (PPI), with eight PPI subscales: Machiavellian egocentricity, social potency, cold-heartedness, carefree non-planfulness, fearlessness, blame externalisations, impulsive nonconformity and stress immunity. The PPI has been tested in a noncriminal population, although the undergraduate samples used raises the question of generalisability to management populations (Lilienfield & Andrews, 1996).
- *The Dark Triad Dirty Dozen*, a 12-item measure of the triad of narcissism, Machiavellianism and psychopathy (Jonason & Webster, 2010).

ORGANISATIONAL INTERVENTIONS

In many countries, workplace health and safety legislation holds employers responsible for ensuring the psychological, emotional and physical wellbeing of employees (Brough, Raper & Spedding, 2020). If it is proven that an employer has breached this responsibility, stress compensation claims may be lodged by affected employees. Therefore, there are both legislative and financial reasons for organisations to effectively manage the occupational stressor of destructive leadership.

When destructive leadership is identified, organisations have three options: do nothing and pay the price in lost productivity and harm to employee wellbeing; isolate the manager from power over others by limiting their people leadership duties or terminating them; or intervene to set boundaries and consequences for their behaviour. It is difficult to research the efficacy of organisational interventions designed to address destructive leadership, primarily because obtaining access to destructive leaders for research purposes is difficult. Most leaders do not self-identify as destructive, and organisations are generally unwilling to admit that they employ leaders who display destructive behaviours. If access is obtained, ego-centred and Machiavellian leaders are likely to try to manipulate the research processes in order to present themselves in the best possible light, especially if the results of the study are going to be communicated to their own manager or executives. An alternative approach is to recruit followers of destructive leaders to describe the behaviours they experience that cause them harm and to evaluate the interventions they have undergone to address this issue. In this instance, it is also difficult to access data within organisations because employees are often too fearful to participate and/or to be honest about their experiences. As a result, convenience or snowball sampling is often employed to recruit participants independently of specific organisations or after they have left the organisation.

In organisational studies, finding relevant control groups and managing attrition in control and experimental groups over the term of longitudinal studies remains a challenge for all areas of research (Brough & Hawkes, 2019). Often, the pros and cons of organisational interventions are discussed in the business and academic literatures, rather than testing their efficacy through rigorous research (Burgess, Brough, Biggs & Hawkes, 2020). Practical organisational interventions that aim to prevent destructive leadership include providing organisations with suggested strategies to constrain destructive leader behaviour (e.g., diagnostics, stringent selection processes, governance frameworks, policies and sanctions), shaping a culture that is not conducive to destructive leadership, enhancing leadership development programmes with activities designed to protect leaders from derailing (e.g., leadership style profiles, resiliency training, reflective practice, self-regulatory mechanisms) and strategies to protect employees from destructive leadership (e.g., stress management interventions, wellbeing and resilience programmes).

Cultural interventions

Executive visibility and manager vulnerability are two factors that have been purported to shape a culture that discourages toxic management styles (Brown, 2018). Executives are required to scan for good conduct, recognizing and rewarding it, and notice bad conduct, calling it out, putting in place boundaries and appropriate consequences for misconduct. To build a culture that protects employee wellbeing, organisations require evidence-based, practical interventions to assist managers to lead at their best and for employees to enhance their wellbeing by becoming resilient to occupational stressors, including the stressor of destructive leadership behaviours by managers (Brough, Wall & Cooper, 2021; Daniel, 2020).

Leader selection interventions

When engaging in a selection process, screening out unsuitable candidates is the most effective way of preventing destructive leadership. Assessing candidates via multiple measures may guard against a poor selection. As destructive leaders are likely to be charming and self-enhancing at interviews, a combination of interviews, leadership self-report inventories (with guards against faking), simulations and/or assessment centre activities over an extended period of time are likely to be more effective in identifying potentially harmful characteristics in candidates.

However, caution has been advised when screening for maladaptive personality traits using personality assessment for selection or development in a workplace environment. This book focuses on the prevalence of destructive leadership traits within a normal organisational population. While profiles based on DSM-IV personality disorders may be appropriate as research tools for investigating destructive leadership in experimental settings, when using assessment to predict specific dysfunctional work behaviours, it may be safer for practitioners to refrain from using scales or composites named after an existing clinical diagnosis, such as those outlined in the DSM-IV (American Psychiatric Association, 1994). Researchers and practitioners instead are advised to select inventories with item content that refers directly to behaviour at work. Yet, as was discussed above, most dark side inventories continue to link their scales to the DSM-IV criteria for personality disorders. This presents a potential risk: utilising clinically based measures to identify destructive leaders, even when designed for normal populations, may allow the perpetrators to claim a lack of responsibility for their behaviours, explaining their behaviour away as characteristics of an innate personality disorder. In addition, if aspects of a personality disorder are implied by an assessment carried out as part of a recruitment and selection process, the assessment may be deemed a medical examination by the courts, preventing it being used as part of the applicant screening process prior to selection. Therefore, the use of a valid assessment that is developed with a normal population and is not based on DSM-IV/DSM-V criteria is recommended as being potentially more appropriate (Christiansen, Quirk, Robie & Oswald, 2014; Judge & LePine, 2007).

Leader development interventions

If there are indications that there is an issue of destructive leadership among existing managers, then a self-report or 360-degree feedback mechanism may be used to raise managers' self-awareness of their dysfunctional behaviours and may also form the basis of leadership development training, mentoring and coaching interventions (Day, Fleenor, Atwater, Sturm & McKee, 2014). However, multi-rater feedback should also be used with caution when it is suspected the leader is demonstrating dark triad tendencies. First, their own assessment is unlikely to be aligned with others' views of their leadership and they may react to feedback in a hostile manner. Second, raters may be too fearful to be honest or may use the tool to 'get at' the leader. Third, the leader may be so focused on trying to guess which rater said what that they ignore the overall themes in the feedback.

For development purposes, leader profile feedback includes both bright side and dark side characteristics, with a focus on when the leader may overdo their strengths. For example, when debriefing a profile, very high levels of achievement drive or independence may result in derailment when the leader is under extreme pressure to achieve results quickly. Debriefing leadership profiles that include both bright and dark side characteristics, such as Dimensions or a combination of Hogan's HPI/HDS, commences with an exploration of the leader's strengths, a discussion on what their triggers are, when they may overdo their strengths and what the impact of that might look like, their self-regulation preferences (i.e., self-awareness, emotional control and stress tolerance traits) and other leadership development opportunities identified in the profile. The HDS is typically debriefed in conjunction with the *Hogan Personality Inventory* (HPI), identifying the leader's daily preferences, and the *Motive Values Preferences Inventory* (MVPI), identifying their motivations and drivers of behaviour. Self-reflection and coaching are common interventions to assist a leader to leverage leadership profiles to increase their self-awareness and to choose to implement behavioural change based on the feedback received. Leader interventions are discussed in more detail in Chapter 10.

Follower interventions

In relation to managing employees' occupational stress as a result of destructive leadership, three key processes are recommended: (a) *preparing employees for stress experiences* – that is, the provision of training interventions to better prepare followers to identify and deal effectively with destructive leadership behaviours and the provision of clear guidelines for escalating problems, lodging grievances and formal complaints, (b) *minimising the risk of stress exposure*, via the removal of leaders who regularly demonstrate destructive leadership behaviours and demonstrate no desire to change and (c) *providing support for exposed employees*, including formal support systems (e.g., EAP, counselling services and workplace conferencing) (Webster & Brough, 2015; Webster, Brough & Daly, 2016). Target and follower interventions are each discussed in detail in Chapters 11 and 12.

CONCLUSION

In this chapter, we have discussed the need to employ valid and reliable diagnostics to identify the risk of destructive leadership and toxic cultures. Diagnostic profiles help clarify a leader's predisposition to engage in destructive leadership behaviours and help inform leader intervention designs. The success of organisational interventions depends on the extent to which the organisation's culture supports the implementation of interventions that prevent and address destructive leadership and protect employees from harm.

10

PRACTICAL IMPLICATIONS FOR LEADERSHIP DEVELOPMENT PROGRAMMES

CHAPTER OVERVIEW

One strategy to help reduce the prevalence of destructive leadership in existing and future leaders is introducing leadership development programmes as an organisational intervention. These work by increasing individuals' self-awareness of their impact and enhancing their self-management skills. Implementing leadership development initiatives also sends a strong message about the organisation's expectations of leader conduct. This chapter reviews the key features and implications of evidence-based leadership development interventions.

PRACTICAL IMPLICATIONS FOR LEADERSHIP DEVELOPMENT PROGRAMMES

When you consider the volumes of resources and finances invested by organisations in leadership development initiatives, it is clear why it is important that psychometric profiling continues to be included as part of rigorous selection processes for such programmes, in order to screen out candidates likely to exhibit destructive leadership behaviours. As we have discussed throughout this book, relationships between narcissism, Machiavellianism, subclinical psychopathy and leader emergence have clearly been demonstrated within the leadership research literature. Indeed, leaders with these traits may be viewed as having leadership potential (e.g., they are perceived as charismatic, confident, risk-taking, assertive, competitive), despite having negative performance reviews and low ratings on leadership by peers and subordinates. This provides some evidence of the ability of such individuals to manipulate decision-makers.

Individuals with these traits are likely to perform very well in traditional selection methods (i.e., interviews, executive sponsorship). For those candidates identified to have potential leadership derailers, but not enough to preclude them from the programme, it can be helpful to provide an in-depth debrief of the selection assessment data, primarily to increase the individual's self-awareness of development areas and to identify contexts where their strengths will lead to effective leadership behaviours and the situations where they may over-use their strengths or derail, consequently harming relationships or their own career (Boddy, 2015; Grijalva, Harms, Newman, Gaddis & Fraley, 2015; Kaiser, LeBreton & Hogan, 2015).

LEADERSHIP DEVELOPMENT PROGRAMMES

To develop leadership styles that enhance employee wellbeing, it is recommended that practitioners include two types of training in their leadership development programmes. The first training focuses on developing constructive leadership behaviours, including, for example, values-based, transformational and authentic leadership styles – styles that consider the needs and wants of leaders and followers (Caza & Jackson, 2011; Copeland, 2014; Kouzes & Posner, 2015). Such training might include a session on the *light triad* (versus the dark triad): humanism, faith in humanity and Kantianism, with Kantianism proposed as a contrast to Machiavellianism (Kaufman, Yaden, Hyde & Tsukayama, 2019). The second type of training looks at destructive leadership behaviours and their common outcomes (Einarsen, Aasland & Skogstad, 2007). These are summarised in Table 10.1.

Table 10.1   Leadership development components for enhancing self-leadership.

Component	Activities

Values-based leadership	• What is leadership? Traditional versus shared leadership definitions. Management vs leadership.
	• The light triad of leadership (Kaufman et al., 2019).
	• Values-based leadership theories (Copeland, 2014) – that is, transformational leadership practices (Kouzes & Posner, 2015) and authentic leadership (Caza & Jackson, 2011).
	• Techniques for enhancing self-awareness:
	  o Leadership profile reports
	  o Alignment between personal values and organisational values
	  o Purpose logo
	  o Seeking feedback – what do I need to keep, start, stop doing?
	  o Mindfulness practice.
	• Building personal resiliency (McEwen, 2016).

Component	Activities

Dark side of leadership	• Recognising destructive leadership (Einarsen et al., 2007).
	• Leader derailment – that is, overdoing strengths (Kaiser et al., 2015).
	• The dark triad of leadership (Furtner et al., 2017).
	• Authenticity paradox (Nyberg & Sveningsson, 2014).
	• Building self-regulation:
	   o Recognising personal triggers – that is, SCARF model (Rock, 2008)
	   o Triggering process – that is, cognitive behavioural models (Edgerton & Palmer, 2005; Neenan & Palmer, 2006)
	   o Having difficult conversations without triggering (Brown, 2018; Scott, 2002).
	• Power and leadership (Hogg & Reid, 2001).
	• Team dysfunctions (Lencioni, 2006).

Leadership development programmes should include mechanisms to enable managers to increase self-awareness of the impact of their leadership style and hold up the mirror to any blind spots they may have. Understanding their triggers, and their capacity to effectively self-manage their impulsivity when triggered, can be enhanced through activities such as self-reflection journaling. Providing a mentor who can facilitate learning from failures and mistakes can also reduce psychological distress for participants, if leaders are actively willing to learn (Boies, Robinson & Robertson, 2010; Kaiser et al., 2015). Leaders also need to be able to reconcile wanting to be an authentic leader with the discomfort of trying new ways of leading and behaving in ways that may not feel genuine or may not yet feel successful to them (Ibarra, 2015; Nyberg & Sveningsson, 2014). An essential component to ensure leaders utilise their strengths while self-regulating impulses that may lead to derailment is building leaders' ability to deal with negative emotions (King & Rothstein, 2010). The more that leaders can deal with frustration, thwarted personal goals and failure effectively, the less likely they are to employ destructive leadership behaviours.

There are several different resilience-building strategies, such as mindfulness techniques, reframing of thinking and mindset and ways of coping with uncertainty, that enable leaders to better deal with negative emotions. These strategies help leaders to employ self-regulation tactics when under stress or fatigued, and allow them to respond effectively, instead of reacting in a way that may cause harm (Atkins, 2008; McEwen, 2016; Moran, 2011). It has also been found that engaging in moderate levels of physical exercise buffers the relationship between supervisor stress and abusive behaviour, so including physical exercise components into leadership development programmes may also be beneficial (Burton, Hoobler & Scheuer, 2012). Teaching and coaching advanced interpersonal communication skills is also important. The resulting improvement in managers' ability to build effective relationships with their staff and garner the support and co-operation of their workforce is, in turn, likely to reduce managers' stress levels and, therefore, their pre-disposition to employ destructive leadership behaviours (Sparks, Faragher & Cooper, 2001).

Factors to maximise leadership development programmes to achieve and sustain the desired results include focusing on the behaviours that really mat-ter (based on the organisational context), ensuring sufficient reach across the organisation (e.g., that the organisation's leadership model reaches all levels), designing the programme for the transfer of learning (e.g., encouraging leaders to practice new behaviours that contribute to their being a better leader and dealing with real problems in a specific context) and using system reinforcement to lock in change (e.g., executives modelling desired leader-ship behaviours, adapting HR systems to reinforce the leadership model) (Feser, Neilsen & Rennie, 2017).

CASE STUDY: 'PRACTICAL PEOPLE MANAGEMENT' LEADERSHIP DEVELOPMENT PROGRAMME

Drawing on the scientific evidence linking leadership styles and behaviours with work performance and psychological health outcomes for their team members, a leadership development programme was developed to assess and improve leadership styles. The programme was called 'practical people management' and was developed and trialled with the collaboration of one Australian police service. The programme was developed to directly incorporate key scientific principles to demonstrate causation and to also assess the cost-benefits of the programme:

1. The programme consisted of 'training' and 'control' groups of leaders, to directly compare the impacts of the training.

2. All participants were assessed pre, during and post programme, to assess training impacts over time.

3. The content of the programme was informed by (a) the scientific literature to ensure that reliable and validated psychological measures and methods were included and (b) previous research conducted with this police organisation, which resulted in the production of tailored police-specific measures of leadership and organisational constructs.

4.   Leadership impact was assessed by multiple sources: self–reports by the leader and team member's assessment of their leaders.

5.   Finally, the programme consisted of multiple components: (a) psychological health and wellbeing surveys, (b) leadership assessments, (c) leaders training workshops, (d) leaders action research projects and (e) leaders individual coaching sessions.

The content of the leadership training was designed to improve leaders' skills in effective people management. Ten common topics of people management were addressed, including, for example, *managing ethical considerations*, *managing conflict* and *providing employee feedback*. These topics have been identified as the most difficult people management areas for leaders to perform well in. A novel component of this programme was the provision of the leaders' individual results to each leader, consisting of their own leadership assessments, their team members' assessments of their leadership and their team members' psychological wellbeing. In this way, we demonstrated any differences between their own perceptions of their leadership (usually very positive) and their team members' assessments of their leadership (usually much less positive), and the impact this difference had on their team members' psychological wellbeing and work performance.

This leadership development programme successfully demonstrated improvements in the leaders' confidence and skills for each of these 10 topics of people management. Transfer of these skills to their workplaces was achieved by the action research project, where the leaders identified a current problem occurring within their team and applied their newly acquired people-management skills to resolve this issue. Leaders were assisted in this problem resolution by their colleagues within the leader workshops and also via individual coaching sessions. Post-training assessments indicated that for the majority of the leaders, their team members' assessments of their leadership had significantly improved, and also had a flow-on effect by improving their team members' wellbeing and work performance (e.g., reduced occurrence of sick days).

This leadership development programme was part of a larger research study with this police service and the results have been disseminated in a number of academic journal articles, written up in the book *Improving criminal justice workplaces: Translating theory and research into evidence-based practice* (Brough, Brown & Biggs, 2016), and featured within a recent book chapter entitled 'Occupational stress and traumatic stress', which appears in the book *The Cambridge handbook of forensic psychology* (Brough, Biggs, Brandon & Follette, in press). For example, in the article by Biggs, Brough and Barbour (2014a), some of the research results emerging from this leadership development programme were presented, specifically demonstrating how the programme improved components of the psychosocial work context for these participants – illustrated in Figure 10.1.

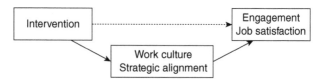

Figure 10.1 Leadership intervention and the psychosocial work context.

Source: Biggs et al. (2014a).

Thus, it can be seen from Figure 10.1 that we aimed to demonstrate how the intervention could produce changes in the participants' perceived psychosocial work characteristics (work culture and strategic alignment), which would in turn impact their psychological outcomes of work engagement and job satisfaction. Importantly, this research study demonstrated that the leadership intervention produced direct effects on levels of work engagement and job satisfaction (illustrated by the dotted line in Figure 10.1). Additionally, the leadership intervention also had significant indirect effects (mediation) by improving the participants' work culture and their sense of strategic alignment with their organisation, which in turn then improved their levels of work engagement and job satisfaction (illustrated by the solid lines in Figure 10.1). By designing this intervention with quasi-experimental scientific research design principles, it demonstrated the significant effects of the intervention over time for the leaders and their team members, and it also demonstrated that improving the quality of exhibited leadership behaviours impacts their employees' psychosocial work characteristics to improve employees' psychological health, motivation and job attitudes.

LEADER COACHING

The transfer of learning from leadership programmes to leader behaviours in the workplace can be enhanced when leader coaching is incorporated into the programme. As part of a leadership development initiative, coaching can assist the coachee to understand their implicit mental models or schemas and identify faulty assumptions that lead to self-defeating strategies or engagement in counterproductive behaviours. Participants may be coached through mindset change to replace faulty mental models and counterproductive behaviours with more constructive alternatives (Gaddis & Foster, 2015; Kaiser et al., 2015). Developing self-regulatory strategies requires commitment by the individual leader to an ongoing cycle of practice, feedback, reflection and guidance. Therefore, before investing time and money into developing a leader with significant potential derailing traits, an assessment of the individual's motivation to engage in ongoing self-development should be conducted. It is recommended that this be combined with an assessment of whether the leader is likely to be able to deploy the newly learned strategies in the workplace, or whether they are more likely to use the tactics learned to manipulate the coach, their manager and their followers, and to better mask their dark side (Diller, Frey & Jonas, 2020; Nelson & Hogan, 2009). However, coaches and practitioners should bear in mind that not all dark side traits lead to derailment. In some contexts, leaders with moderate to high levels of these traits are successful, at least within the short term. For example, leaders with unusually high self-confidence and risk-taking, who are attention-seeking and gregarious but less inclined to be agreeable, tend to be more successful in sales roles. These same characteristics may also make them very difficult to manage. Leaders with narcissistic tendencies are likely to be successful in business, in entrepreneurial or senior executive roles and may be seen by others as having the courage to act (Furnham, Trickey & Hyde, 2012).

Derailing leaders, those who overdo their strengths (e.g., through extreme achievement drive or a strong need for harmony/avoidance of conflict), may benefit from coaching based on acceptance commitment training (ACT). This coaching seeks to increase psychological flexibility and change the relationship that coachees have with their thoughts, feelings and inner experiences. It allows individuals to be able to sit with discomfort, rather than suppress negative emotion (Collis, 2013; Moran, 2011). This frees leaders up to choose to behave in line with their values. It is important that they freely choose their values, not just choose values they feel they *should* have. Working with their true values encourages the leader to take action that is in their long-term best interest and mitigates somewhat against actions that are rewarding in the short term but unworkable in the long term. ACT coaching techniques include:

- drawing their purpose logo
- values inventory
- mindfulness activities
- gratefulness diary
- perspective taking

- reflective journaling
- resilience building
- Goal Reality Options Will (GROW) for committed action.

Should an organisation decide to hire or promote a candidate with extreme derailing personality traits, perhaps due to the individual's rare technical expertise and skills, additional support and professional development strategies will be required during their on-boarding, such as providing coaching by a psychologist, to prevent engagement in destructive leadership behaviours. There has been some support for the proposition that psychologist coaches are more likely to effectively assist managers with skill application and setting behavioural change goals (Bono, Purvanova, Towler & Peterson, 2009).

LEADER INTERVENTION

Alternatively, an organisation may have investigated a leader's conduct and want to intervene. There are a number of reasons why organisations may feel they cannot intervene themselves: they did not see or hear the conduct being complained about, they do not have enough evidence of misconduct, they fear dealing with the individual's defensive/defiant/resistant response, they believe the individual will be litigious or they believe that the leader cannot change. In this situation, the best approach may be to offer coaching that focuses on the leader's reputation and the negative perceptions of their leadership style that are being generated in those around them. Coaching should not be mandated. Mandating coaching is likely to lead to more resistance from the leader or to the leader just giving lip-service to the coaching programme so the problem will go away. When taking up coaching, it is the coachee's choice whether to engage or not in the process. No-one can force a leader to engage in leadership development initiatives. However, if they do not engage and the misconduct continues, the organisation must be prepared to follow through and enact the previously stated consequences.

For 'abrasive leaders', those managers who rub people up the wrong way, Crawshaw (2010) proposed an action-research method for coaching, based on the reputational damage or negative perceptions of co-workers in response to the leader's conduct. The steps for action-research coaching are summarised in Table 10.2. As many abrasive managers tend to be unaware of the impact of their leadership style, it is important to raise their awareness without also triggering their defensiveness. Therefore, Crawshaw proposes three steps: planning, action, fact-finding.

Table 10.2   Process for coaching 'abrasive leaders'.

Steps	Activities
Planning	• Data gathering of negative perceptions (through co-worker interviews). • Anonymised feedback of findings (to the abrasive leader). • Collaborative analysis of motivation behind client's abrasive behaviours that produce negative co-worker perceptions. Analysis is conducted through the lens of the *Threat>Anxiety>Defence* dynamic.
Action	• Applying the *Insight Cycle*, coach asks the leader to develop hypotheses on why the leader's behaviours generate negative perceptions. Coach the client and then develop and test insight-driven strategies to achieve leader's objectives without generating negative perceptions.
Fact-finding	• Approximately three months after coaching has begun, the coach re-interviews the client's co-workers, this time to gather their current perceptions. This second cycle of fact-finding provides updated information on whether the client's actions have extinguished negative perceptions about their conduct. The leader may learn that the negative perceptions are not entirely eradicated, and this finding leads into another iteration of the action-research and coaching process (e.g., planning, action, fact-finding).

Source: Adapted from Crawshaw (2010).

When engaging in the planning step, data can be gathered from a range of sources, including leader profiles, multi-rater feedback, observations of the leader in team meetings or when working with the team and analysing the organisational systems and environment within which the leader operates (e.g., what behaviours and practices are rewarded and what are sanctioned). The coach seeks to understand interpersonal dynamics and will take advantage of any opportunity to personally witness social interactions. From a systemic perspective, the coach believes it is important to look beyond the behaviour of the leader in order to understand events (e.g., interactions between the leader, followers and conducive environments). Indeed, the coach must be aware that their own beliefs, mindset and actions also influence the coaching process (Lawrence, 2019). This coaching approach acknowledges that different people have different perspectives on a situation, and so they will have different versions of what needs to happen next. Therefore, people need to work together to come up with a plan of action. Once action has been taken, the leader then seeks further feedback as to the extent to which these actions have addressed negative perceptions about their leadership and, depending on the feedback received, may then engage in another cycle of planning, action and fact-finding.

Before bringing in external specialists/coaches, however, it is important to note that the organisation has a role to play in the intervention – namely, clearly articulating expectations of leader conduct, evaluating their conduct and holding leaders to account for their behaviour. This responsibility cannot be outsourced and, fundamentally, no leadership development or coaching programme will be successful without the organisation taking action first to send a clear message on their expectations of leaders. Therefore, experts invited in to deal with issues of destructive leadership typically take on a consultant role and work with the organisation to ensure all steps have been put in place prior to implementation, to maximise the success of the intervention.

The key factors considered by leadership specialists when designing a leader intervention include the history of the problem, whether it is a long-standing issue and what action has been taken to date. The organisation must be willing to allow employees to be interviewed or surveyed to gather information and data about the problem. It is not the leadership specialist/coach's role to convince the leader that there is a problem, that they indeed are the problem or to motivate the leader to be willing to solve the problem. If a leader is to engage openly with an external party, then confidentiality needs to be maintained; so, for example, progress reports back to the organisation are not appropriate. Instead, the leader is encouraged to share the outcomes of coaching/leadership development activities directly with their manager. In summary, coaches and leadership specialists are not miracle workers. A leadership intervention can only be effective if the organisation's structures, systems and actions support the intervention (Crawshaw, 2010).

CONCLUSION

Leader and leadership development programmes are key strategies for articulating expectations for leader conduct, preventing leaders engaging in destructive leadership behaviours, encouraging leaders to enhance their awareness of the impact of their leadership style and upskilling leaders in self-management techniques, so that they avoid derailment. Importantly, effective leadership development programmes can also positively influence the broader psycho-social working context for all employees, resulting in improved employee wellbeing and work performance. Thus, in this chapter, it has again been made clearly apparent how leaders set the work context 'tone' for their workers. Leader coaching complements leadership development programmes, through helping leaders' change their mindsets and enhancing their ability to change derailing behaviours by adopting new, constructive leadership styles.

11

PRACTICAL IMPLICATIONS FOR FOLLOWER INTERVENTIONS

CHAPTER OVERVIEW

Despite all that can be done to prevent harm to employees (i.e., targets, followers, third-party observers), destructive leadership remains an ongoing problem in organisations. This chapter discusses evidence-based practices and processes, key methodological principles and common difficulties in design-ing interventions to address and help protect employees from the harm of destructive leadership.

PRACTICAL IMPLICATIONS FOR FOLLOWER INTERVENTIONS

Experiencing positive, supportive relationships with direct managers can sig-nificantly offset workplace stressors and reduce stress experiences. Conversely, experiencing aversive relationships and negative interactions with manag-ers is a significant cause of occupational stress (O'Driscoll & Brough, 2010). While acknowledging the occurrence of good and supportive managers, it remains true that many managers are likely to instigate negative interactions with followers that create stress. Therefore, instead of focusing purely on try-ing to change the behaviour of the offending leader, whether intentional or not, it is equally important to improve the personal resiliency and coping skills of the potential targets of destructive leadership behaviours. A review of the *stress management intervention* (SMI) literature for dealing with occupational stress is useful in order to determine ways of reducing the harmful effects of destructive leadership and enhancing employee wellbeing (Burgess, Brough, Biggs, & Hawkes, 2020; Webster & Brough, 2015). SMI design is embedded in a tripartite framework that describes three levels of SMIs: *primary prevention*, organisational interventions to eliminate stressors from the work environment and prevent stress, *secondary prevention* interventions, detecting stress and providing stress management skills, and *tertiary prevention* interventions to rehabilitate stressed workers (Brough, O'Driscoll, Kalliath, Cooper & Poelmans, 2009). Table 11.1 provides examples of primary, secondary and tertiary prevention SMIs in the context of destructive leadership.

Table 11.1 Stress management interventions (SMIs) in the context of destructive leadership.

Interventions	Example strategies
Primary interventions (prevention)	• Leadership development programmes
	• Documented code of conduct
	• Whistleblowing policy
	• An effective risk-identification and monitoring system for complaints
	• A contact point for advice and access to confidential counselling
	• Addressing destructive behaviours promptly
	• Removal of leaders demonstrating ongoing destructive leadership behaviours
Secondary interventions (protection)	• SMIs, focusing on protecting employees (targets and bystanders) by building the personal resiliency, career resilience and coping skills of employees
	• Wellbeing programmes
Tertiary interventions (addressing harm caused)	• Safe-reporting mechanisms
	• Mediation and conflict resolution
	• Team coaching
	• Workplace conferencing

PRIMARY PREVENTION INTERVENTIONS

Primary prevention interventions focus on the direct elimination or reduction of stressors from the work environment. This may include increasing work resources to address the problem (e.g., providing more personnel or finance), sanctioning or removing the destructive leader or establishing policies, procedures and practices that promote employee wellbeing (see Table 11.1). Despite most organisations having robust primary prevention strategies in place, the prevalence of destructive leadership behaviours in workplaces remains a common issue.

SECONDARY PREVENTION INTERVENTIONS

SMIs

To date, much of the SMI research has focused predominantly on secondary prevention SMIs for individuals. Cognitive-behavioural programmes are reported as producing among the largest effect sizes in reducing distress, at least in the short term (Brough & Boase, 2019). There is limited evidence of individual interventions producing long-term effects (Giga, Noblet, Faragher & Cooper, 2003; Lamontagne Keegel, Louie, Ostry & Landsbergis, 2007; Richardson & Rothstein, 2008; van der Klink, Blonk, Schene & van Dijk, 2001). Stress management training (SMT) is moderately effective in improving employees' psychological health (Flaxman & Bond, 2010a). Resilience-building programmes also demonstrate some efficacy (e.g., Brough & Boase, 2019; Pipe et al., 2012).

To maximise their effectiveness, SMIs work best within organisations with strong governance frameworks and explicit organisational support for well-being programmes (primary prevention) and effective mechanisms to support staff after a stressful interaction (tertiary interventions). It is also important that SMI interventions have a sound theoretical base. Four theoretical approaches relevant to designing an effective *secondary prevention* SMI are stress-inoculation training (SIT; Meichenbaum, 1996), positive psychology techniques (Seligman & Csikszentmihalyi, 2000), acceptance and commitment training (ACT) techniques to build personal resilience (Burton, Pakenham & Brown, 2010; Harris, 2009) and career management strategies to increase perceptions of personal control and enhance career resilience (Vuori, Toppinen-Tanner & Mutanen, 2012). We summarise the common approaches for effective SMIs below.

SIT

To date, the concept of SIT has been utilised in organisations to mitigate the effects of psychological and emotional distress as a result of stress, burnout and/or physical injury (Saunders, Driskell, Johnston & Salas, 1996). SIT assists individuals to cope with the aftermath of exposure to stressful events and to 'inoculate' them against future and longer-term stressors (Meichenbaum, 1996). The principles used in SIT may be useful for building employees' awareness of the potential harm resulting from destructive leadership behaviours – for example, education focused on employee recognition that they may become a target of such behaviours, and what techniques they can employ to develop resiliency and prevent or minimise psychological, emotional and/or physical harm.

In essence, an intervention to inoculate them against the effects of destructive leadership. SIT techniques include increasing knowledge and awareness of stress triggers, providing reading materials, problem-articulation skills, describing emotions likely to be experienced on the job, focusing on the transient nature of unpleasant situations, conflict resolution and self-regulatory training. While SIT is still used to treat individuals working in high-stress occupations or work environments (Meichenbaum, 2017), organisations have now moved to resiliency training as part of their wellbeing programmes. Table 11.2 sets out the phases of SIT as it applies to addressing the impact of destructive leadership.

Table 11.2   Phases of stress-inoculation training (SIT) applicable to destructive leadership.

Phases of SIT	
Conceptualisation phase	• Establish a collaborative relationship between employees and the trainer
	• Educate employees about the nature and impact of the stress (e.g., how to recognise specific destructive leadership behaviours)
	• Encourage employees to identify and view the perceived threat as a problem to be solved
	• Help employees to distinguish between which elements of the problem they may be able to change and those which they cannot (which is especially useful with destructive leadership)
	• Teach employees to set specific short-, medium- and long-term coping and resilience-building goals
Skill-acquisition phase	• Education (e.g., follower style)
	• Skills practice (i.e., emotional self-regulation, cognitive restructuring, problem solving, using social support systems, acceptance of uncomfortable emotions)
Application and follow-through phase	• Help employees to identify high-risk situations and warning signs to prevent harm (e.g., to identify destructive leadership behaviours when they occur and plan mitigation strategies)
	• Encourage employees to help others with similar problems (social support)

Measuring resilience at work

Self-assessment of personal resilience is an important aspect of building resilience and may be included as a pre/post measure for an SMI. For example, the R@W scale measures seven components of resilience at work based on cognitive-behavioural principles and seeking social support: living authentically, finding your calling, maintaining perspective, mastering stress, interacting co-operatively, staying healthy, and building networks (McEwen, 2016).

Building resiliency - Positive psychology techniques

Positive psychology, founded by Martin Seligman (Seligman & Csikszentmihalyi, 2000), is a cognitive-behavioural approach primarily concerned with using psychological theory, research and intervention techniques to understand the positive and adaptive aspects of human behaviour, especially in relation to reducing anxiety and depression resulting from stress. Positive psychology strategies are designed to help individuals change their negative styles of thinking in order to positively impact their feelings, even in situations where they experience negative emotions and/or helplessness. Tactics include reviewing components of personal life satisfaction, identifying personal values and signature strengths and using mindfulness techniques to stay in the moment, rather than ruminating about the past or worrying about the future (Brown, Ryan & Creswell, 2007; Burton et al., 2010; Gander, Proyer, Ruch & Wyss, 2012). A review of 15 studies examining the effects of positive psychology interventions in organisations indicated that these interventions enhanced employee wellbeing and decreased levels of stress and anxiety (Meyers, van Woerkom & Bakker, 2013).

Building resiliency - ACT

ACT, a cognitive-behavioural and mindfulness-based approach, draws on a range of techniques designed to increase psychological flexibility and facilitate values-based action. ACT promotes six core processes to increase psychological flexibility and resilience: (a) choosing *acceptance* rather than avoiding negative emotions; (b) *cognitive defusion*, changing the interaction with thoughts to defuse the believability of unhelpful thoughts; (c) *self-observation*, being aware of one's thoughts and experiences without attachment to them; (d) *being present* or mindful so an individual can experience the world more directly, in the moment, rather than ruminating about the past or worrying about the future; (e) using personal *values* to drive purposeful action and (f) *committed action* aligned to personal values (Collis, 2013; Flaxman, Bond & Livheim, 2013; Moran, 2015). Three common ACT techniques that provide affected employees with the opportunity to choose a constructive response to destructive leadership include practising mindfulness exercises to increase present moment awareness and reduce the struggle with undesirable and aversive thoughts and emotions, completing a values inventory and completing an action plan to facilitate clarification of goals and actions. Furthermore, it has been found to be particularly beneficial for participants experiencing psychological distress, with one study demonstrating that both SIT and ACT have been found to be equally effective in reducing psychological distress at work (Flaxman & Bond, 2010a, 2010b).

Interventions based on cognitive-behavioural principles are more effective when combined with techniques to increase individuals' personal resources (Brough & Boase, 2019; Richardson & Rothstein, 2008). While most SMI programmes include cognitive-behavioural techniques to build personal resilience and often include a goal-setting component, there are few research studies assessing the efficacy of training programmes to improve career resilience and career wellbeing.

Building career resilience

In contrast to the literature on career success and satisfaction, less attention has focused on what happens when careers go badly. Engaging individuals in their own career development is one strategy to increase personal resources, subsequently reducing workplace stressors. For example, Kidd (2008) reported in a study of 89 UK workers that the most common negative career experience was interpersonal difficulties with their manager, such as working for an aggressive, undermining or unsupportive boss. These negative career experiences produce negative emotions, including dejection, anxiety, frustration and feelings of worthlessness. Workplace interpersonal conflicts and harassment (instigated by both managers and colleagues) remain as the key workplace stressors commonly experienced by a variety of workers today (Brough, Raper & Spedding, 2020). Given the impact destructive leadership often produces on employees' careers and job satisfaction, career management skills are likely to enhance followers' personal resources and, as a result, their sense of control. Individuals high in career resilience have improved resistance to career disruptions in suboptimal environments and are better able to cope with strong emotions. A lack of support in building career resilience can result in dysfunctional coping strategies when confronted with career barriers (London, 1997).

Career resilience interventions focus on encouraging individuals to take responsibility for their own career management in an unpredictable work environment. Career resilience is enhanced by training interventions that help individuals interpret career barriers accurately, deal with negative emotions and formulate coping strategies that remove the barriers, by reframing their ideas, repositioning their energies and/or changing career direction (London, 1997). Career resilience training may assist individuals with their sense-making when facing adverse career experiences (e.g., the ongoing process through which individuals attempt to make sense of the circumstances in which they find themselves and determine how the situations affect them). Career management strategies thus assist workers to evaluate their choices and choose an appropriate response (Burton, Webster & Lees, 2010; Zellars, Justice & Beck, 2011). Vuori et al. (2012), for example, reported on a group training intervention focused on enhancing individuals' career management skills. Their training intervention had a positive impact on both career resilience and mental distress. Training components that enable followers to improve their career management skills (e.g., identifying their strengths, obtaining career-related resources and learning concrete ways to manage their own career), as well as inoculate them against career barriers (e.g., enhancing their abilities to anticipate setbacks and to adjust to their work environment), are valuable techniques when dealing with the stress of destructive leadership. Without career management skills, followers are likely to 'unwillingly stay' in their job, which can result in long-term harm to their wellbeing (Webster, Brough & Daly, 2016).

Due to the psychological, emotional, physical and career harm as a result of being subjected to destructive leadership behaviours, an intervention that draws on a combination of SMT techniques, based on theoretical foundations of cognitive-behavioural therapy, SIT, positive psychology, ACT, resiliency and career resilience, is highly recommended. This multi-discipline approach increases the efficacy of interventions to improve employee wellbeing by enabling participants to become more resilient to destructive leadership behaviours (see Table 11.3).

Table 11.3   Theoretical basis for secondary prevention stress management intervention (SMI).

Intervention component	Underpinning theoretical framework	Example
Collaborative facilitator relationship with participants	SIT (Meichenbaum, 1996)	Facilitator demonstrates appreciation of workplace context and understanding of culture
Destructive leadership	SIT (Meichenbaum, 1996)	Education on nature and impact of the stressor; indices to recognise values-based versus destructive leadership and its impact Education on effective/ineffective coping tactics for dealing with destructive leadership, skill acquisition, identifying mitigating strategies, setting coping and resilience-building goals
		Managing up – what sort of follower am I? Focus on what participants are able to control/change

(Continued)

Table 11.3 (Continued)

Intervention component	Underpinning theoretical framework	Example
Personal resiliency	Resiliency (McLarnon & Rothstein, 2013; McEwen, 2016)	Definition of resiliency
	Positive psychology (Seligman & Csikszentmihalyi, 2000)	Self-assessment measures of resiliency: resilience at work, positive emotions, signature strengths, values, meaning and purpose
	ACT and mindfulness (Brown et al., 2007; Collis, 2013; Harris, 2009)	Education on ACT and mindfulness techniques; skill acquisition
Career resilience	Career resilience (Kidd, 2008)	Definition of career resilience; self-assessment measures of career resilience; action planning
Social support	Support seeking (Yagil et al., 2011; Webster et al., 2016)	Reflection activity on social networks and support; encourage employees to support each other
Application and follow-through	SIT (Meichenbaum, 1996)	Interactive sessions and group discussions to encourage peer learning; action plan to transfer learnings to the workplace

CASE STUDY

A quasi-experimental research study was conducted within a healthcare setting to evaluate the effectiveness of a secondary prevention SMI to improve wellbeing in the context of reduced employee satisfaction in part due to destructive leadership behaviours being demonstrated in the workplace (Webster, 2016). The organisation where the research was conducted had a values-based leadership framework, a code of conduct, policies and procedures for dealing with unacceptable behaviour and a disciplinary management process in place. Tertiary interventions were also available to staff, via counsellors, chaplains and an employee assistance programme.

The experimental group took part in a four-hour resiliency training session. The focus of the intervention was on increasing participants' confidence in their ability to manage their own personal and career resilience generally and, specifically, when confronted with abusive leadership behaviours. The approach incorporated psycho-education (SIT), cognitive-behavioural skills training (ACT and mindfulness skills), career resilience strategies and group facilitation techniques to allow participants time to process and apply learnings to their situation and workplace – for example, self-reflection on own stressors and coping strategies and identification of work-related problems in relation to abusive leadership experiences through group discussions and pair activities. The theoretical underpinnings of this intervention are listed in Table 11.3.

Participants were assisted to understand their own follower style, as well as their personal values, motivations, fears and needs. Maladaptive responses to fear triggers or unmet needs were explored. Strategies for building career resilience to enhance job satisfaction and employability, irrespective of work environments and situations, were included (e.g., understanding career phases, aligning work with participants' own values and sense of purpose and a review of work/life integration). Strategies for building personal resilience and techniques that are useful when managing setbacks, and to deal appropriately and assertively with them as they arose, were also provided. Mindfulness exercises, based on ACT principles to create a happier, more satisfying life, were introduced (e.g., gratitude exercises, health and wellbeing evaluations, reviewing social support networks). The facilitator created a supportive learning environment and led interactive sessions that encouraged peer learning by allowing participants to discuss obstacles and share experiences. The facilitator promoted mindset change, as opinions and insights were challenged by other group participants. Participants identified their own work preferences, lifestyle and career-related goals, defined tasks for carrying out these goals and practised the required actions in small groups. Participants completed a *Building Resilience Action Plan* to take away with them.

Twenty workshops were facilitated over six months, with 186 healthcare employees attending the workshops and 178 of these employees participating in a research project. Participant attendance at workshops was maximised by offering short, four-hour sessions, scheduled at times that fitted in well with shifts. A control group was included in the study design but, due to attrition over time, was not of a sufficient sample size to be included in the research project data analysis. The impact of the workshops was evaluated over three-months. Participants reported significantly increased knowledge, motivation and confidence to employ learned resiliency-building strategies in the workplace immediately after the training session. Participants also reported significantly increased psychological and affective wellbeing three months after the final resilience training session. The results of this intervention provide some support for the utility of a brief secondary stress prevention intervention in assisting employees to prepare for and/or deal with destructive leadership behaviours in a way that maintains wellbeing.

TERTIARY INTERVENTIONS

After destructive leadership incidents have been identified, a number of employees are likely to have already been targeted, with significant negative impact on their wellbeing. Tertiary prevention interventions are designed to rehabilitate stressed workers. Typical organisational interventions include formal investigations, counselling and mediation. Interventions such as providing employee assistance programs and counselling support may be useful in addressing the effects of harm caused by destructive leadership, at least in the short term. However, employees are often reluctant to access organisation-recommended services for fear their confidentiality will be breached. Complementary interventions, such as workplace conferencing, offer an alternative to traditional approaches.

Formal investigations

Taking a legalistic, industrial relations approach to cases of witnessed gross misconduct (e.g., sustained extreme cases of destructive leadership and abusive behaviours by a manager) can be effective through a process of investigation, warning, discipline, sanction and/or dismissal. However, from a practitioner's point of view, a typical approach to complaints against managers, irrespective of their scale and scope, is to immediately commence with a formal investigation. This causes immense stress to all parties: the accused manager, the complainant target and employees interviewed within the investigation process. This is especially problematic when the behaviour complained about has happened behind closed doors, without witnesses, or is the subject of hearsay. Whether the complaint is upheld or not, it is difficult, if not impossible, for those going through this legal process to be able to work together at the time of the investigation or, if the complaint is not upheld, afterwards. Thus, formal internal investigations may not achieve the resolution or restitution originally sought. Instead, our recommendation is that consideration needs to be given to creating a more humanistic approach to dealing effectively with destructive leadership behaviours, in a manner that clearly prioritises the psychosocial safety of employees.

Mediation

There is some debate about the suitability of mediation and conflict resolution in the context of destructive leadership. There are certainly some risks of using mediation interventions in this context (Bennett, 2013). Mediation that brings the manager and target together, as accused and accuser, may not be appropriate considering the inherent power differential between these two stakeholders. Confidentiality in mediation can never be absolute and mediators are bound by a duty of care to ensure the safety of either participant. Strategies to manage the power relationships between the parties includes holding individual sessions, allowing the complainant to be accompanied by a support person, utilising conflict coaching, making sure both parties are aware of their rights during the mediation process and reality testing available options for the parties should the mediation not be successful. Psychological support is essential for severely traumatised targets. It is suggested that if the parties do engage in mediation, this should not be the sole intervention. Additional ways of supporting the manager and complainant are required to complement traditional approaches (e.g., leader coaching, employee counselling, employee assistance programmes) and/or alternative approaches (e.g., workplace conferencing).

Team coaching

Once a destructive leader is removed, it often takes the team some time to recover. Some team members may feel guilty about their manager losing their job as a result of their complaint. Other team members may feel guilty about not speaking up when they observed or experienced destructive leadership behaviours. It is recommended that within a couple of weeks of the manager leaving, the team be brought together for team coaching with an external coach. This provides a safe place to discuss what has happened and for each worker to share their individual experiences and thoughts. The team can re-contract team ground rules and agree how they will work together in future. If a new manager has been appointed, this also provides them with a valuable opportunity to participate in the re-contracting process.

Workplace conferencing

Workplace conferencing is based on restorative justice principles (Thorsborne, 2014). This process may allow organisations to identify ways to prevent harm occurring in the future, while supporting the complainant target/s and minimising the risk of being liable to litigation or compensation claims. With a skilled facilitator, this process provides a safe environment for each party to relate their experiences, to discuss what happened, to describe the impact of the harmful behaviours and to explore whether there is a way forward that can ensure the future psychosocial safety and wellbeing of affected employees. Interventions based on restorative justice principles are discussed in more detail in Chapter 12.

EFFICACY OF SMIs

It is difficult to find a compromise between administering an effective intervention that includes appropriate theoretical components via an optimal research design and one that facilitates active participation in an intervention that fulfils organisational requirements and is sponsored by the executive (Nielsen, Taris & Cox, 2010). Individual interventions still dominate the SMI literature, and these interventions may also include group training sessions (Richardson & Rothstein, 2008). However, interventions with a preventative focus have had limited evaluations of their outcomes, and any reported effects of the intervention on outcomes have been small (Brough & O'Driscoll, 2010; Burgess et al., 2020). This is primarily due to the challenges in conducting SMI research within organisations (Brough & Biggs, 2015). Implementing data collection activities in the workplace is often inconvenient and there can be many constraints to address, for example, accommodating shift workers, or releasing staff from operational duties to attend the intervention programme. Higher participation rates are achieved by holding the intervention on-site; however, this can also lead to interruptions when employees are called away from sessions for work reasons (Biggs & Brough, 2015a).

Active, direct and clearly apparent support for any intervention from both executive and local managers (champions) is critical for effective participation and implementation of the intervention (Biggs & Brough, 2015b). However, executive organisational priorities can change over the duration of a longitudinal study, and competing projects may occur, altering the level of support initially provided to the study. Commitment from employees is required for successful data collection, especially for longitudinal designs, when there are often varying interests across different parties. It can also be difficult to find a control group for comparison, especially if relying on third-party managers to recruit participants. Wait-listed control group participants may feel data collection is too demanding when they are not participating in the intervention, even if they will receive the programme at a later date. Alternatively, it may not be ethical to keep the control group waiting for the intervention long enough to carry out longitudinal analyses. These factors often negatively affect the ability to include a control group or to ensure adequate control group sample sizes within organisational research projects.

To address potential barriers, interventions must be designed to be practical, highly relevant to the workplace and as interactive as possible. Teams with high levels of manager support are more likely to be encouraged to implement the intervention back in the workplace and this can mediate the effect of the intervention. However, this may be difficult, of course, if the manager's behaviour is the actual stressor. External factors that have been identified as difficult to control in studies include the need for executive sponsorship to implement an organisation-wide intervention, the executive team insisting on choosing the departments/teams they wish to participate in the intervention, managers selecting employees for participation and the readiness of the individuals selected to use the skills learned (Brough & Biggs, 2015; Pipe et al., 2012). The effectiveness of interventions to assist followers to manage the stressor of destructive leadership must be formally evaluated in order to demonstrate any actual long-term benefits. Attention has also been drawn to the importance of evaluating both micro processes (e.g., increased participant resilience and wellbeing) and macro processes (e.g., participant attendance and participant appraisal of the quality of the intervention), when evaluating the implementation (Biggs & Brough, 2015a).

CONCLUSION

Interpersonal conflict within workplaces, including conflicts arising from managers' behaviours, unfortunately remains a common occupational stressor. This chapter has reviewed and discussed several evidence-based SMI programmes that are appropriate for implementation in the context of destructive leadership. Multiple, complementary approaches are most valuable to effectively address the complexity of this issue. The numerous obstacles that can hinder the efficacy of destructive leadership SMI programmes should not deter researchers from continuing to investigate the effectiveness of these programmes within the workplace. Planning routes around these obstacles and ensuring any intervention programme is formally evaluated to demonstrate return on investment will increase the long-term success of these programmes.

12

REPAIRING THE DAMAGE CAUSED BY DESTRUCTIVE LEADERSHIP

CHAPTER OVERVIEW

As we discussed in Chapter 11, traditional responses to counterproductive behaviour by managers may not be effective in the context of destructive leadership. Often, organisations need to look beyond grievances, formal investigations, mediation or conflict resolution to address the impact of destructive leadership. This chapter considers an alternative intervention for repairing the harm caused to targets and observers by destructive leadership, and how workplace conferencing (a form of restorative justice) can be an effective solution, or at least a complementary intervention.

REPAIRING THE DAMAGE CAUSED BY DESTRUCTIVE LEADERSHIP

Interventions to build coping skills and resiliency to stressors can assist in reducing current adverse personal experiences and prevent future harm, as we discussed in Chapter 8. However, many employees may already have experienced destructive leadership practices during the course of their career, causing significant negative impacts on their psychological, emotional and physical health, especially if such events have not been acknowledged and validated (Lipman-Blumen, 2005; Mehta & Maheshwari, 2013). As we discussed in Chapter 11, primary, secondary and tertiary interventions can each be useful to address the harm caused by this extreme workplace stressor. However, evidence suggests the success of tertiary interventions (e.g., employee assistance programmes (EAPs)) is often limited, especially for any long-term solutions.

There is limited research into the efficacy of EAPs in the long term and a lack of knowledge about the range of work issues being reported. The outcomes most commonly studied are absenteeism, presenteeism and level of functioning at home and at work, with less research describing the outcomes of health and wellbeing (Berridge, Cooper & Highley, 1992; Joseph, Walker & Fuller-Tyszkiewicz, 2018). As discussed previously, targets of destructive leadership are often reluctant to engage in EAP services provided by the organisation where the abuse is occurring (Webster, Brough & Daly, 2016). Overall, the literature suggests scarce research has been conducted into how organisations address the negative impacts of destructive leadership for workers 'after the fact' (e.g., Kellerman, 2004; Lipman-Blumen, 2005). One approach that has been considered to address the significant harm caused by exposure to destructive leaders is *workplace conferencing*, based on a restorative justice approach (Thorsborne, 2014).

A common approach to addressing conflict in workplaces is to consider the situation as a formal grievance or complaint and refer it to internal investigation (Brough, Lawrence et al., in press). The extent to which grievance procedures restore employee perceptions of justice in the workplace has been questioned, especially in situations where they perceive they have experienced unjust treatment from a leader (Bemmels, Brown & Read, 2009). Often, these incidents are complex, with conflict based on a non-linear continuum of different staff members' stories across time. In the context of destructive leadership, such internal processes presume the source of the conflict is between the manager and the staff members who are parties to the conflict. In doing so, the investigation may be limited in its effectiveness, as a focus only on individuals excludes any consideration of the role that organisational factors play in creating and maintaining this conflict. The target experiences stress as a result of the manager's 'bad behaviour' and, more significantly, from not being supported by the organisation to address the bad behaviour. As discussed in previous chapters, the failure of senior management and human resources (HR) to consistently enforce the formal systems for addressing bad behaviour, such as the code of conduct, anti-bullying policy and disciplinary procedures, leads to an increase in conflict. What is preferable is a problem-solving approach that considers the whole organisational environment in order to effectively deal with the sources and maintenance of the conflict. If investigations, grievances, dispute resolution or mediation make matters worse when dealing with workplace conflict resulting from destructive leadership, then what other options are there?

One alternative dispute resolution (ADR) response is *group conferencing*, which brings together the parties affected by destructive behaviour in the workplace, providing the opportunity to consider the impact of workplace culture on the situation (Curtin, 2018; Jülich & Cox, 2013; O'Sullivan, 2017). Principles of restorative justice have been applied to workplace dilemmas, for example, when dealing with conflict or broken relationships in a workplace context, addressing internal staff complaints and grievances and/or inappropriate behaviours from employees and managers as they arise (Faldetta, 2019; Goodstein & Aquino, 2010; Okimoto & Wenzel, 2014). A restorative justice approach suggests that if an action or behaviour caused hurt, then an effective response must be healing. Numerous people can be hurt by an incident of destructive leadership, not just the direct target. The leader themselves, observers, family members, colleagues and the wider organisational community may also have been affected by the incident/s. A restorative approach considers the broader context and identifies the conditions that allowed an incident to happen and to be maintained. Restorative practices offer those who have been harmed the opportunity to have this hurt acknowledged through dialogue and to be involved in how they would like amends to be made. Restorative justice processes achieve accountability by considering multiple individual- and organisational-level perspectives and by looking to the future, to identify what must be done to repair trust and relationships (Dekker, 2017; Dekker & Breakey, 2016).

This approach is also referred to as 'transformational justice' when it can achieve more than simply restoring the individual to the way they were before the harmful incidents. Transformational justice may also create a healing and developmental experience for all involved individuals (Hopkins, 2015; Liebmann, 2007). Restorative justice does not nullify the social or legal obligations of the organisation; instead, it offers alternative forms of accountability that avoid direct blame. Workplace conferences have been successfully conducted to deal with inadequate and abusive management and bullying in organisations, including abusive supervision at, for example, a television station, a coal mine and in schools (Branch & Murray, 2015; Hopkins, 2015; Moore, 1996).

WORKPLACE CONFERENCING

Based on a restorative justice approach, the underpinning philosophy of *workplace conferencing* is that it allows the participants to gradually shift their focus from the past, to the present and the future, and to also improve their emotional state to a point where they can acknowledge and 'transform' the conflict. Everyone affected is encouraged to attend these conferences and each is given the opportunity to speak. No party is able to block another from attending, speaking or being listened to. Instead, all contributions are listened to and given due consideration. The guiding principles of restorative justice focus on transparency (about all aspects of the process), clarity (communicating in a way that enables comprehension of conferencing principles and processes) and respect (for all participants). The facilitator's role is to identify the source of the conflict in a system of relationships, bring the impacted individuals together in a circle of discussion and dialogue, invite the participants to respond to open questions in order to assist the parties to better understand the incidents or issues that have contributed to the conflict and finally to safeguard the process (i.e., not allow any party to highjack the agenda) as the participants work through the transformation of conflict (Jülich & Cox, 2013; Meyer, 2011; Moore, 1998, 2004). When a collective picture has been identified of what has happened and how individuals have been affected, the facilitator creates a space for all to reflect on the experience. There can be a profound emotional turning point when participants begin working constructively towards a plan of action for making the situation better in the following weeks or months.

As outlined in Table 12.1, there is much groundwork to be done by the facilitator prior to the conference commencing, in terms of obtaining a brief, conducting a group briefing and participant interviews and analysing the data to identify the key incidents, issues and conflicts. While some pre-conference interviews may be conducted virtually, if necessary, workplace conferences are best conducted in face-to-face situations. Following this groundwork, workplace conferences involve introducing the conference, allowing all the participants to tell their story, exploring and acknowledging the harm that has been caused, developing a plan for the future to resolve the issue, recording the plan and then closing the conference, ensuring all participants are satisfied.

Table 12.1 Workplace conference process.

Stage	Activities
Groundwork	• Brief – establish the purpose of the workplace conference, a range of alternative outcomes and the preferred outcomes.
	• Group briefing – arrange a time with the identified participants who will be involved in the workplace conference to explain what is going to happen. This group briefing must be attended by management.

(Continued)

Table 12.1 (Continued)

Stage	Activities
Pre-conference interviews	• Conduct pre-conference confidential interviews with all participants.
	• Collate the data from the interviews to create an issues list and discuss these with management, including the problematic behaviours that are contributing to the issues/conflict.
	• Report key themes/issues (no detail is necessary) that have been identified back to staff involved in the interviews (if possible).
	• Develop a seating plan for the conference (in a circle with no table present).
Workplace conference – Introduction	• Remind participants of ground rules and check everyone agrees with rules of engagement.
	• Invite each participant to share why they want the process and what outcomes they are hoping for.
	• Telling the story and exploring the harm – ask each person in turn to share with the group their general experiences of the workplace.
	• Then share with the group the key incidents/issues that have been identified. Ask each person who had a role in the incident to respond to pre-prepared questions (depending on whether they are the one responsible for the incident or the target). For those responsible, the purpose of the questions is to establish motivation and intent, and the individuals' awareness of the impact of their behaviour. For those harmed, the purpose is to explore the harm and the damage done to relationships.
Workplace conference – Acknowledging the harm	• Ask questions of each person to help them reach a shared understanding of the harm that has resulted from the incidents/issues.
Workplace conference – Developing a plan	• The target/complainant can be asked, 'What would you like to see happen that will make things right for you?'
	• If a change of behaviour is requested of the person responsible, check in with that person to see if they think the request is fair and appropriate and if they will commit to the request.
	• Ask all other participants, 'What ideas do you have to improve the situation? What is your personal commitment to the plan?'
Workplace conference – Recording the plan	• Ask the group how they wish the plan to be recorded.
Closing the workplace conference	• Once the group is satisfied with the recorded plan, ask 'Before we close, is there anything else anyone wants to say?'
	• Thank them for their participation and commitment to the process.
	• If feasible, ask each participant to read and sign the terms of the agreement, and as each person leaves, hand them a copy.

Source: Adapted from Thorsborne (2014).

Note: Workplace conferencing must be conducted by external, experienced workplace conferencing facilitators. Having two facilitators is recommended (e.g., provides two perspectives and allows them to facilitate and observe group dynamics/conflicts more effectively).

Destructive leadership produces increased intra-team and inter-team conflict. For example, leaders can play favourites to encourage in-group out-group distinctions and to create interpersonal conflicts and competition within and between teams. In the USA, Fitzgerald (2006) pioneered the use of *corporate circles* (up to 20 participants per circle) to build trust in organisations by addressing conflict in teams, resolving disputes and rebuilding damaged workplace relations. Corporate circles are designed to manage and reduce conflict between team members. Corporate circles, like workplace conferences, bring together those people who are affected by abuse or bullying to have courageous, candid and compassionate conversations with the goal of transforming conflict. The circles focus on providing a safe environment, where team members feel safe to share their perceptions about what has been happening in the workplace, explore hidden causes for the conflict, express their emotions safely (even strong negative emotions, such as shame or disgust) and explain how they have been impacted. Through open dialogue, the group discusses how best to repair any harm, and how to prevent future interpersonal conflict from occurring. The goal is for participants to learn as a group how to resolve any future conflict, for example, by practising the skills of empathetic and active listening, paraphrasing or mirroring, using the body to communicate understanding and by staying silent. Fitzgerald (2006) suggested that corporate circles directly assist the process of rebuilding trust by re-establishing connections between co-workers and engaging in activities that allow them to demonstrate their trustworthiness.

WORKPLACE CONFERENCING IN THE CONTEXT OF DESTRUCTIVE LEADERSHIP

There are several pertinent issues to consider when taking a restorative approach to managing conflict in the workplace as a result of destructive leadership. Margaret Thorsborne has been practising workplace conferencing for many years, including addressing harm caused by destructive leadership incidents. We include here an interview with Margaret Thorsborne below, together with case studies from her workplace conferencing practice.

Interview with Margaret Thorsborne, workplace conferencing practitioner:

What are the pros and cons of restorative approaches versus traditional workplace mediation?

'In my opinion, mediation is a bit limited because it is usually between two opposing parties and it never, in its purest form, allows an expansion to include the rest of the community that may have been affected by what has happened. I would much rather use restorative processes for this reason, than do a mediation between only a few. If the parties are willing, and there has been an acceptance of responsibility – conflict is often co-constructed – then in many instances responsibility for what went wrong is shared amongst the parties involved.

Mediation seeks to keep the emotions out of it, to stay in the rational mode. However restorative work intentionally asks clients how they have been affected and what has been the worst of it. This elicits responses that are descriptions of the emotional impact of the problem. The advantage of a restorative approach is that it widens the community of people who should be included. It seeks a reduction in symptoms of trauma – to help people move out the other side. The key in the workplace is to keep small things small; don't let them fester. People need to be heard. They need to have their stories validated.

> One more consideration here is to realise that the person responsible will also need healing. If you are that person in the workplace who has made the mistake, you will also need to recover from the mistake and the harm you've caused, a chance to explain how and why it happened, so you too can move on. This requires a level of conflict competence – to see opportunities in the conflict to strengthen relationships, to understand how it affects you and others, and to know what to do.'

What are the key principles that underpin workplace conferencing?

'Restorative processes are based on the principles: 1. Inclusive decision making (the people who are affected by the problem need to be involved in the problem solving); 2. Active accountability (bringing all affected people together to do this work face-to-face in the room); 3. Repairing the violations of people and relationships (asking questions such as 'How has this harmed you? What are your needs in terms of having things made right?'), and finally, 4. Rebuilding trust (Karp, 2019).

> You set the tone by starting the conference with thanking the parties for agreeing to come and saying, "This is an opportunity to see if we can make sense of what has happened. It is not about whether anyone is good or bad. It is about us trying to understand what has happened and the harm that has been done, to see what we can do to make things better". During the conference you can ask the parties to reflect on things such as: "Think

about the ways in which you have let your work colleagues down. Think about what you value about your work colleagues". This I learnt from my colleague Ruth Levy, a restorative mediator who works with intractable conflict situations in workplaces, with great success.

When you have a closed community, such as a workplace, whether it is a team in a school, a real estate agency, a law practice, or a government department, people experience conflict in the same ways everywhere. They suffer the same wounds. The loss of trust I think is one of the worst parts of unresolved conflict. We are wired to live in right relationships with each other and we feel the disconnections keenly. It can be devastating for our sense of who we are, for productivity and teamwork. People get so distressed with unresolved conflict (usually caused by many factors), that it can become a Workplace Health and Safety issue.

Whatever approach you take to dispute or conflict resolution, you will have to manage the risk as to whether you do something, and what that is, or whether you do nothing. If a destructive leader who has caused harm is not willing or capable of engaging in a restorative process, then the "walking wounded" can be brought together with senior people from the organisation to address the harm caused without the person responsible being present. This will assist more senior people understand the impacts of the difficult behaviour on the workplace and may signal a clear direction that needs to be taken. In my experience of people who have difficult or high conflict personalities, it is almost impossible to work with them restoratively, because they are not prepared to accept criticism or negative feedback. There are furthers harms perpetrated when a "high conflict" personality is unable or refuses to accept responsibility for a situation where they clearly have had a role. Whatever process is chosen, it's important to remember that we are working with people who are already harmed – do no more harm.'

Below are the three case studies Margaret shared with the authors (www.thorsborne.com.au).

Case Study 1: Transformative for the Leader and Those Affected

This case involved the poor performance of a partner in a law firm, and the problems that arose as a result of a culture of silence about matters that desperately needed airing. As soon as the staff and partners became more accustomed to speaking openly in a climate of safety, the issues that had assumed such huge proportions were quickly resolved.

I was approached to resolve an almost total breakdown in communication between a senior partner in a law firm and one of the lawyers who worked in the same division. The problems stemmed from early misunderstandings in their working relationship and were quickly resolved. In interviewing them prior to the conference, it became apparent that deeper problems existed in the organisation, particularly between the partners who had not been frank with each other about issues that really mattered, despite yearly retreats at which they developed strategic and business plans. With some trepidation, the whole partnership allowed a process of exploration of these deeper issues. It became clear that one particular partner had not been performing for some time, was not meeting business targets and, as a result, was causing feelings of deep resentment with the other partners and staff.

The managing partner, with help, was able to broach the concerns to the non-performing partner, who was able to shed some light on these issues. They, finally, were also able to admit to him that they wished to terminate the current relationship of partner with him, but retain his services (which were highly regarded, despite his lack of focus). After some initial reluctance, which was overcome by an offer to buy his partnership, he agreed to relinquish the position and finally accepted the offer with an increasing sense of relief. The partners had some other issues to sort out but agreed that they were well on the way to managing these, having finally experienced helpfulness of emotional honesty and how important it was to keep the firm focused.

Case Study 2: Restorative Approach to Grievances

This case illustrates how dissatisfying formal complaint processes (grievances) can be and how much damage they can do in a workplace, on top of the already damaging aggressive behaviour exhibited by a manager who was the subject of the complaints.

Pre-conference interviews with staff at a public sector office revealed deep dissatisfaction at the outcomes of two recent grievances that had been lodged against the previous manager, who had been moved to another (temporary position) within the government agency. While he had been much respected by staff for his intellectual and operational skills, he had exhibited behaviours that deeply troubled them. Staff were upset by his behaviours and the response from management when they complained. Staff felt they had been kept in the dark about the outcomes of their grievance and had not been sufficiently supported through the processes.

There were allegations of a cover-up by senior management raised by a staff member who went on stress leave, and he was keen to lodge a grievance against senior managers because of this alleged 'cover-up'. He was asked to hold off on a final decision on this, until after this workplace conference. Most staff were keen for him to drop the whole idea of lodging a grievance, believing that he was too distracted by it, enough was enough and they wanted to move on.

Interviews revealed that staff were extremely worried about the impact on their careers if they spoke honestly during the conference, believing that at some future date, 'pay-back' was inevitable. Interviews also revealed the office was alive with rumours that resulted in increasing levels of anxiety, anger a, and cynicism about management's role in the whole circumstances.

The conference began with a reminder that the purpose of the day was to reach a shared understanding of the harm that had been done over time, and to come to some agreement about how to repair that harm and move forward. Participants were also reminded that anything they said during the conference was without prejudice and could not be used in any way against them in some future action. The conference then dealt with the incidents and issues that had so deeply affected staff since their first attempt to get help to deal with the manager's behaviour. These included:

- senior management's failure to take concerns expressed by staff on many occasions seriously,
- how the grievance investigations were conducted,
- whether the manager who had moved on was receiving any counselling regarding his performance,
- the alleged 'cover-up' by senior management and
- how the staff felt about the prospect of another grievance.

The agreement reached during the conference included a stay on the decision to move ahead with the next grievance, closer involvement by the district manager with the staff at this office and greater consultation with them. Two further conferences were conducted at two monthly intervals as follow-up, to ensure that both staff and senior management were satisfied with the outcomes and the office was functioning efficiently and without the distraction of further conflict. A new manager was finally appointed, which resulted in a few teething problems, but early intervention resolved these early difficulties.

Case Study 3: Transformative for Those Affected, After the Leader Left

This case illustrates the enormous damage created in a workplace by a highly toxic manager. The damage was so profound that his departure from the company was not enough to heal the wounds and further action was required to repair relationships between all those affected by his behaviour.

This case arose as the result of the resignation of a financial controller from a factory. Senior management, in their keenness to modernise the financial processes within administration, had hired an accountant on the recommendation of a well respected recruitment organisation. He came to the job with good technical and systems skills, and quickly hired staff who were young, ambitious, highly skilled and who subsequently became extremely loyal to him. Unfortunately, his approach to other staff who had been with the company for some time, and who wrestled with the bedding down of the new systems he put in place, was aggressive, rude, contemptuous and downright nasty. He made lewd comments about their private lives, threatened some with job loss and told one female, long-term employee that she was 'too old and too ugly' and that he was going to get rid of her.

These staff, not unexpectedly, despite their fear of him, began to complain quietly to management. When the volume of complaints reached a level that could no longer be ignored, management employed an industrial relations consultant to investigate the claims. Management was convinced the problem was serious, and after several interviews with him, invited him to seek employment elsewhere. This news was greeted with relief by the staff who had suffered abuse, but with outrage by the staff who were loyal to him, who blamed the 'old-timers' for not being able to cope with new approaches and for moving to have him sacked.

A conference brought the two groups, along with senior management, together. This allowed all parties to be told the full story of the financial controller's resignation, how he had impacted so negatively with his approach and how diminished staff had become. Older staff listened to the disappointments and blame levelled at them by those loyal to him, while this latter group finally understood the scope of damage that had been done. Management was also criticised by both groups for failing to move more quickly on the problems as they emerged.

The frank and sometimes painful disclosures at the conference brought all parties to a deeper understanding of the harm done and gradually individuals and groups began to experience themselves as 'we' instead of 'them' and 'us'. Agreements reached reflected the need for greater care to be taken with recruitment and selection and alterations to, and development of, systems within the organisation that protected workplace relationships. Great care was taken to hire a person who had effective people management skills as the next financial controller.

Case Study 4: Deciding When Not to Proceed

This case illustrates that there are times when, in the interests of doing no harm, the best decision is not to proceed. The individual concerned was reported as being very difficult to work with, to the extent that people were afraid of what they felt she was capable of doing. Everyone affected by her toxic behaviours was interviewed, and then the individual herself was interviewed. It became clear during the interview that this individual had some aspects of a serious personality disorder, undiagnosed. As a result, it was decided not to continue with the conference due to the risk for the parties. Instead, it was recommended the workplace be assessed for the workplace health and safety risk to staff due to stress created by the toxic leader and the likelihood of WorkCover mental injury claims. A significant number of staff were identified as being at high risk of not being able to continue at work for much longer, given the stress levels they were experiencing and exhibiting. The findings of the workplace assessment highlighted the need to remove the individual, who was paid out and left.

As demonstrated in these case studies, there are some risks associated with using interventions based on restorative justice principles in the context of destructive leadership that need to be managed. For example, organisations are unlikely to replace legalistic approaches, such as grievance processes, with restorative approaches (Paul, 2017). More likely, they will import them into the existing system, creating potential tensions between legalistic processes that aim to hold the wrongdoer accountable with sanctions and, as discussed above, restorative justice processes that aim to achieve accountability by encouraging the wrongdoer to accept responsibility and apologise, possibly offering reparations with the person/people who were hurt (Fehr & Gelfand, 2012).

When the target and offender come from different levels of the organisational hierarchy, the imbalance of power requires skilful facilitation. One key principle of restorative justice is that the destructive leader makes admission of the offending and takes responsibility for their actions. If this does not happen, the target can feel abused again and further harmed. Where it is deemed by the facilitator that there is a risk the leader will not admit offending, accept accountability for their behaviour or express remorse for their actions, three options are open: choose not to proceed with the workplace conference; facilitate indirect conferencing between the parties, without a face-to-face meeting; or facilitate a workplace circle between executive management and the target (excluding the destructive leader), with the organisational community accepting responsibility for the harm the organisation has caused through the destructive behaviour of the manager and exploring ways to prevent it happening again.

Nor is workplace conferencing a quick or cheap fix. For conferencing to be successful, extensive resources, time and commitment are required from management, a lot of time must be invested from the parties involved and extensive preparation and follow-up actions are required by the facilitator before and after the conference is convened (Goodstein & Aquino, 2010). To date, there is limited research data on the efficacy of restorative justice processes in workplaces, other than the testaments of workplace conferencing practitioners, with most studies based on workplaces in the education sector (Jülich & Cox, 2013; Hopkins, 2015; Paul, 2017). More case studies and longitudinal research investigations are required to understand how this process works across different industries, workplaces and cultures and to test the sustainability of the results.

CONCLUSION

This chapter has discussed how traditional responses to destructive leadership in organisations may miss the mark when addressing the harm caused or even unintentionally create more distress to those affected. Interventions based on restorative justice principles present an alternative, complementary approach to conflict or dispute resolution and stress-prevention interventions. Workplace conferencing can be conducted as an alternative to an investigation, or after an investigation, to restore working relationships. Workplace conferencing warrants further research in the context of addressing the consequences of destructive leadership.

13

DESTRUCTIVE LEADERSHIP: FUTURE DIRECTIONS FOR RESEARCH AND PRACTICE

CHAPTER OVERVIEW

In this book, we have tackled the complex problem of destructive leadership in the workplace from a range of perspectives, at individual, group and organisational levels. This chapter brings together the key learnings, practical implications and points of interest that have been raised throughout this book. We also discuss the next steps and future directions in the area of destructive leadership, both for researchers and practitioners.

KEY LEARNINGS CONCERNING DESTRUCTIVE LEADERSHIP

The preceding 12 chapters in this book have presented a broad discussion of the multiple definitions of destructive leadership, key antecedents, common impacts and consequences, key enablers and the evidence-based interventions employed to reduce the occurrences and impact of destructive leadership (Chapter 1 provides a summary of each chapter). It is clear that there are multiple reasons why managers behave badly, although overdoing their specific personality characteristics or reacting impulsively due to their various insecurities explain many of the sources of their bad behaviour. It is also clear that there are negative consequences for the leader themselves and for their targets as a result of their engaging in destructive leadership behaviours.

Employers have a duty of care to provide psychologically safe working environments for all their workers, and this includes protection from exposure to bullying, harassment and abuse from managers and colleagues. Specific characteristics of large organisations, in particular, can obstruct this protection and we have discussed how organisational cultures and employee silence can work to hide, maintain and even foster destructive leadership behaviours. It is apparent that destructive leaders produce both short-term and long-term damage for their targets, work groups and the productivity and profitability of their organisations. While recent progress has been made to better manage destructive leaders and the damage they cause internally, it still remains the case that either efficiently removing this leader from the organisation or their targets removing *themselves* from the organisation remain the most effective ways to actually stop these damaging experiences. In either case, the loss of skilled employees is rarely good news for an organisation and it is clear that better practices for identification during selection, leader development and rehabilitation of abusive leaders remain a pressing requirement.

We have also discussed the role of targets in the toxic leader/employee dyads and the mechanisms by which harm is caused to targets and third-party observers. We critiqued organisational stress management interventions designed to build employees coping skills and resiliency and improve team functioning in the context of destructive leadership. We suggest that more respectful and humane processes for dealing with destructive leadership, and protecting the psychosocial wellbeing of employees, are required if employers are to effectively discharge their duty of care to their workforce.

NEXT STEPS FOR THE IMPROVED MANAGEMENT OF DESTRUCTIVE LEADERSHIP

Recent social changes have produced less tolerance for bad behaviours exhibited either at work (e.g., via the #*MeToo* initiative) or at home (e.g., increased intolerance of domestic violence). This is, of course, good news and has directly and indirectly assisted to reduce the stigma long associated with the identification and reporting of inappropriate work behaviours, including bullying and harassment perpetrated by managers. This decreased stigma has resulted in a recent increased number of reports of workplace bullying and harassment, which is also good news. Fewer managers are now 'getting away with' behaving badly and more employees are emboldened to report the occurrence of any such behaviours. However, this has now produced a bottleneck in the effective management of these destructive workplace behaviours, due to a lack of effective evidence-based interventions and of skilled practitioners with appropriate experience to lead these interventions. Consequently, this is one reason why claims of employee mental ill-health have increased in recent years in this area, as we discussed in the preceding chapters. This increase has been exacerbated further by the COVID-19 pandemic. During times of economic uncertainty, many organisations reduce their professional development and wellbeing initiatives, and, consequently, improvements to workplace practices focused on supportive people management practices typically falter, just at the time when employees need such initiatives the most.

What is occurring is increased recognition of the need for effective ways to support employees through the pandemic and in response to the emerging different ways of working, including the issue of remote supervision. For some targets of destructive leaders, the pandemic and the necessity for working remotely has been a relief, primarily due to the physical avoidance of their manager. However, what remains currently unknown is how exactly destructive leadership has transformed itself with the onset of remote working. For some targets, remote working has resulted in increased monitoring and micromanaging of their work time and their performance and unreasonable supervisory demands. There may also be an increase in one-on-one direct supervision between the manager and their target, as opposed to team-based supervision. This direct one-on-one supervision, even when conducted remotely, can remain highly destructive for the target. Some targets are taking opportunities to record such adverse occurrences, and the release of these recordings internally to senior managers and/or externally to social media channels can force senior managers' action to remedy the situation.

FUTURE DIRECTIONS FOR RESEARCH

Throughout this book, we have discussed the advances that have occurred in identifying and managing specific components of destructive leadership behaviours. However, it is also apparent that there remain specific components that require further consideration and research to better protect employees. This includes, for example, the assessment of dysfunctional coping strategies that targets do not wish to report they engage in. We know some targets engage in avoidance and numbing options through substance abuse or engage in displaced aggression leading to domestic violence of targets' families. Theoretical explanations for the leader–target dyad interaction, such as May, Wesche, Heinitz & Kerschreiter's (2014) theoretical proposition on the impact of levels of targets' submissiveness versus confrontativeness on leader behaviour, would directly benefit from empirical testing, so we can better understand how employees may de-escalate abuse from their manager. There is also a need to improve our understanding of the role of co-workers and bystanders who witness destructive leadership behaviours but who are not the direct targets themselves. It would be useful, for example, to better understand these bystanders' decision mechanisms and what exactly influences their decisions, when they choose to protect or shun the targets of destructive leadership.

At the organisational level, there is still scarce research on the relationship between the organisation's political atmosphere and the occurrence of destructive leadership. Recent research has, for example, discussed how and why destructive leadership can occur in national collective cultures and, especially, the influence of a high power-distance. How to effectively overcome these organisational, national and societal contexts when managing destructive leadership still remains a clear problem. There is also certainly a need for more studies adopting longitudinal research designs to investigate the actual effectiveness of leadership development programmes in reducing the incidence of destructive leadership and the efficacy of interventions addressing the negative impacts of destructive leadership, after harm has occurred. For example, recent studies in the field of workplace wellbeing have identified the value of employees taking micro-breaks from work, and also the role of connecting with nature during work time to reduce experiences of stress and to facilitate wellbeing and work performance (Brough, Wall & Cooper, 2021). We suggest that such wellbeing experiences are also likely to be beneficial in the context of dealing with destructive leadership, although exactly how such initiatives can be best applied in this specific context remains unclear.

We acknowledge that due to people's personalities, background experiences and motivations, the basic situation of people working together is rarely always harmonious. However, there are few justifications for unprofessional and toxic behaviours to occur at work, and especially when such behaviours are conducted in a purposeful and chronically demoralising manner. Our aim in producing this book is to encourage awareness of and discussions on these destructive leadership behaviours, and to highlight the areas requiring more considered assessment by researchers in this field. We certainly hope that current and future workers' tolerance for destructive workplace behaviours diminishes and that toxic leaders unwilling to adapt and amend their ways eventually become the unemployable dinosaurs they deserve to be.

REFERENCES

Aasland, M. S., Skogstad, A., Notelaers, G., Nielsen, M. B., & Einarsen, S. (2010). The prevalence of destructive leadership behaviour. *British Journal of Management, 21*, 438–452.

Akar, H. (2018). Organizational silence in educational organizations: A meta-analysis study, *International Journal of Eurasia Social Sciences, 9*(32), 1077–1098.

Akca, M. (2017). The impact of toxic leadership on intention to leave of employees. *International Journal of Economics, Business and Management Research, 1*(4), 285–290.

Akuffo, I. N., & Kivipõld, K. (2017). Leadership behaviour in the context of nepotism, cronyism, and favouritism: a review of the literature. In S. Morison (Ed.), *Leadership for improvement perceptions, influences and gender differences* (pp. 255–282). New York: NOVA Publishers.

American Psychiatric Association (1994). *Diagnostic and statistical manual of mental disorders. DSM-IV.* Washington: American Psychiatric Association.

Ames, D. R., & Flynn, F. J. (2007). What breaks a leader: The curvilinear relation between assertiveness and leadership. *Journal of Personality and Social Psychology, 92*(2), 307–324.

Ames, D. R., Rose, P., & Anderson, C. P. (2006). The NPI-16 as a short measure of narcissism. *Journal of Research in Personality, 40*, 440–450.

Aryee, S., Chen, Z. X., Sun, L., & Debrah, Y. A. (2007). Antecedents and outcomes of abusive supervision: Test of a trickle-down model. *Journal of Applied Psychology, 92*, 191–201.

Ashforth, B. (1994). Petty tyranny in organizations. *Human Relations, 47*, 755–778.

Atkins, P. (2008). Leadership as response not reaction: Wisdom and mindfulness in public sector leadership. In P. Hart & J. Uhr (Eds.), *Public leadership - perspectives and practices.* Canberra, ACT: ANU Press.

Avolio, B. J., Walumbwa, F. O., & Weber, T. J. (2009). Leadership: Current theories, research, and future directions. *Annual Review of Psychology, 60*, 421–449.

Babiak, P., & Hare, R. D. (2007). *Snakes in suits. When psychopaths go to work.* New York: Harper Collins.

Babiak, P., Neumann, C. S., & Hare, R. D. (2010). Corporate psychopathy: Talking the walk. *Behavioral Sciences and the Law, 28*, 174–193.

Baker, E. L., Boedigheimer, S. F., Moffatt, S., Altman, D., Castrucci, B. C., & Halverson, P. K. (2018). Preventing leader derailment—a strategic imperative for public health agencies. *Journal of Public Health Management and Practice, 24*(4), 400–403.

Bamberger, P. A., & Bacharach, S. B. (2006). Abusive supervision and subordinate problem drinking: Taking resistance, stress and subordinate personality into account. *Human Relations, 59*, 723–752.

Bandura, A. (1991). Social cognitive theory of self-regulation. *Organizational Behavior and Human Decision Processes, 90*, 248–287.

Barbuto, J. E. (2000). Influence triggers: A framework for understanding follower compliance. *Leadership Quarterly, 11*(3), 365–387.

Bardes, M., & Piccolo, R. F. (2010). Goal setting as an antecedent of destructive leader behaviors. In B. Schyns & T. Hansborough (Eds.), *When leadership goes wrong: Destructive leadership, mistakes and ethical failures* (pp. 3–22). Chicago: Information Age Publishing.

Baumeister, R. F., Muraven, M., & Tice, D. M. (2000). Ego depletion: A resource model of volition, self-regulation, and controlled processing. *Social Cognition, 18*(2), 130–150.

Belschak, F. D., Muhammad, R. S., & Den Hartog, D. N. (2018). Birds of a feather can butt heads: When Machiavellian employees work with Machiavellian leaders. *Journal of Business Ethics, 151*(3), 613–626.

Bemmels, B., Brown, G., & Read, R. (2009). *A restorative justice perspective on grievance procedures.* Presented at *15th World Congress of the International Industrial Relations Association*, 24–28 August, Sydney, Australia.

Bennett, T. (2013). Workplace mediation and the empowerment of disputants: rhetoric or reality? *Industrial Relations Journal, 44*(2), 189–209.

Benson, M. J., & Campbell, J. P. (2007). To be, or not to be, linear: An expanded representation of personality and its relationship to leadership performance. *International Journal of Selection and Assessment, 15*(2), 232–249.

Berdahl, J. L., Cooper, M., Glick, P., Livingston, R. W., & Williams, J. C. (2018). Work as a masculinity contest. *Journal of Social Issues, 74*(3), 422–448.

Berridge, J., Cooper, C. L., & Highley, C. (1992). *Employee assistance programs and workplace counseling.* Chichester: Wiley.

Bhandarker, A., & Rai, S. (2019). Toxic leadership: emotional distress and coping strategy. *International Journal of Organization Theory & Behavior, 22*(1), 65–78.

Biggs, A., & Brough, P. (2015a). Explaining intervention success and failure: What works, when, and why? In M. Karanika-Muray & C. Biron (Eds.), *Derailed organizational stress and well-being interventions: Confessions of failure and solutions for success* (pp. 237–244). London: Springer.

Biggs, A., & Brough, P. (2015b). Challenges of intervention acceptance in complex, multifaceted organisations: The importance of local champions. In M. Karanika-Murray and C. Biron (Eds.), *Derailed organizational stress and well-being interventions: Confessions of failure and solutions for success* (pp. 151–158). London: Springer.

Biggs, A., Brough, P., & Barbour, J. P. (2014a). Enhancing work-related attitudes and work engagement: A quasi-experimental study of the impact of an organizational intervention. *International Journal of Stress Management, 21*, 43–68.

Biggs, A., Brough, P., & Barbour, J. P. (2014b). Relationships of individual and organizational support with engagement: Examining various types of causality in a three-wave study. *Work & Stress, 28*(3), 236–254.

Bligh, M. C., Kohles, J. C., Pearce, C. L., Justin, J. E., & Stovall, J. F. (2007). When the romance is over: Follower perspectives of aversive leadership. *Applied Psychology: An International Review, 56*(4), 528–557.

Boddy, C. R. (2011). Corporate psychopaths, bullying and unfair supervision in the workplace. *Journal of Business Ethics, 100*(3), 367–379.

Boddy, C. R. (2015). Organisational psychopaths: A ten year update. *Management Decision, 53*(10), 2407–2432.

Boddy, C. R., Miles, D., Sanyal, C., & Hartog, M. (2015). Extreme managers, extreme workplaces: Capitalism, organisations and corporate psychopaths. *Organization, 22*(4), 530–551.

Boies, K., Robinson, M. A., & Robertson, M. C. S. (2010). Leaders' personal experience and response to failure. A theoretical framework and initial test. In B. Schyns & T. Hansborough (Eds.), *When leadership goes wrong: Destructive leadership, mistakes and ethical failures* (pp. 357–382). Charlotte, NC: Information Age Publishing, Inc.

Bono, J. E., Purvanova, R. K., Towler, A. J., & Peterson, D. B. (2009). A survey of executive coaching practices. *Personnel Psychology, 62*, 361–404.

Branch, S., & Murray, J. (2015). Workplace bullying. Is lack of understanding the reason for inaction? *Organizational Dynamics, 44*(4), 287–295.

Brandebo, M. F. (2020). Destructive leadership in crisis management. *Leadership & Organization Development Journal, 41*(4), 567–580.

Brandebo, M. F., & Alvinius, A. (2019). *Dark sides of organizational behavior and leadership.* London: Intech.

Braun, S. (2016). Narcissistic leadership. In A. Farazmand (Ed.), *Global encyclopedia of public administration, public policy, and governance* (pp. 1–9). Cham: Springer.

Breevaart, K., Bakker, A. B., Hetland, J., & Hetland, H. (2014). The influence of constructive and destructive leadership behaviors on follower burnout. In M. P. Leiter, A. B. Bakker, & C. Maslach (Eds.), *Burnout at work: A psychological perspective* (pp. 102–121). London: Psycholoy Press.

Brinsfield, C. T. (2013). Employee silence motives: Investigation of dimensionality and development of measures. *Journal of Organizational Behavior, 34*(5), 671–697.

Brooks, S., & Wilkinson, A. (in press). Employee voice as a route to wellbeing. In P. Brough, E. Gardiner, & K. Daniels (Eds.), *Handbook on management and employment practices.* London: Springer.

Brough, P. (2005). Workplace violence experienced by paramedics: Relationships with social support, job satisfaction, and psychological strain. *Australasian Journal of Disaster and Trauma Studies, 2005*(2). Retrieved from http://trauma.massey.ac.nz/issues/2005-2/brough.htm (Accessed on 3 November, 2021)

Brough, P., & Biggs, A. (2010). Occupational stress in police and prison staff. In J. Brown & E. Campbell (Eds.), *The Cambridge handbook of forensic psychology* (pp. 707–718). Cambridge, UK: Cambridge University Press.

Brough, P., & Biggs, A. (2015). The highs and lows of occupational stress intervention research: Lessons learnt from collaborations with high-risk industries. In M. Karanika-Murray & C. Biron (Eds.), *Derailed organizational stress and well-being interventions: Confessions of failure and solutions for success* (pp. 263–270). London: Springer.

Brough, P., Biggs, A., Brandon, B., & Follette, V. (in press). Occupational stress and traumatic stress. In J. Brown (Ed). *The Cambridge handbook of forensic psychology* (2nd ed.) Cambridge, UK: Cambridge University Press.

Brough, P., & Boase, A. (2019). Occupational stress management in the legal profession: Development, validation, and assessment of a stress-management instrument. *Australian Journal of Psychology, 71*, 273–284.

Brough, P., Brown, J., & Biggs, A. (2016). *Improving criminal justice workplaces: Translating theory and research into evidenced-based practice.* London: Routledge.

Brough, P., Drummond, S., & Biggs, A. (2018). Job support, coping and control: Assessment of simultaneous impacts within the occupational stress process. *Journal of Occupational Health Psychology, 23*(2), 188–197.

Brough, P., Hassan, Z., & O'Driscoll, M. P. (2014). Worklife enrichment. In M. Dollard, A. Shimazu, R. Bin Nordin, P. Brough, & M. Tuckey (Eds.), *Psychosocial factors at work in the Asia Pacific* (pp. 323–336). London: Springer.

Brough, P., & Hawkes, A. (2019). Designing impactful research. In P. Brough (Ed.), *Advanced research methods for applied psychology: Design, analysis, and reporting* (pp. 7–14). London: Routledge.

Brough, P., Kinman, G., McDowall, A., & Chan, X. W. (2021). '#MeToo' for work-life balance. *Work-Life Balance Bulletin: A DOP Publication, 5*(1), 4–8.

Brough, P., Lawrence, S., Tsahuridu, E., & Brown, A.J. (in press). The effective management of whistleblowing: The Whistleblowing Response Model. In P. Brough, E. Gardiner, & K. Daniels (Eds.), *Handbook on management and employment practices*. London: Springer.

Brough, P., Muller, W., & Westman, M. (2018). Work, stress, and relationships: The crossover process model. *Australian Journal of Psychology, 70*, 341–349.

Brough, P., & O'Driscoll, M. (2010). Organisational interventions for balancing work and home demands: An overview. *Work & Stress, 24*, 280–297.

Brough, P., O'Driscoll, M., Kalliath, T., Cooper, C. L., & Poelmans, S. A. (2009). *Workplace psychological health: Current research and practice.* Cheltenham: Edward Elgar Publishing.

Brough, P., & Pears, J. (2004). Evaluating the influence of the type of social support on job satisfaction and work-related psychological well-being. *International Journal of Organisational Behaviour, 8*, 472–485.

Brough, P., Raper, M., & Spedding, J. (2020). 'She'll be right, mate!' Occupational stress research in Australia. In K. Sharma, C. Cooper, & D. M. Pestonjee (Eds.), *Organizational stress around the world: Research and practice* (pp. 7–22). London: Routledge.

Brough, P., Timms, C., Chan, X. W., Hawkes, A., & Rasmussen, L. (2020). Work-life balance: Definitions, causes, and consequences. In T. Theorell (Ed.), *Handbook series on occupational health sciences* (pp. 473–487). London: Springer Nature.

Brough, P., Wall, T., & Cooper, C. (2021). Organizational Wellbeing: An Introduction and Future Directions. In T.Z. Wall, C.L. Cooper, & P. Brough (Eds.), *The SAGE Handbook of Organizational Wellbeing* (pp. 1–6). London: Sage.

Brough, P., & Westman, M. (2018). Crossover, culture, and dual-earner couples. In K Shockley, W. Shen, & R. Johnson (Eds.), *The Cambridge handbook of the global work-family interface* (pp. 629–645). Cambridge, UK: Cambridge University Press.

Brough, P., Westman, M., Chen, S., & Chan, X. W. (in press). Psychological crossover: Definitions, explanations, and new directions. In P. Brough, E. Gardiner, & K. Daniels (Eds.), *Handbook on management and employment practices*. London: Springer.

Brown, A. J., Lawrence, S., Olsen, J., Rosemann, L., Hall, K., Tsahuridu, E., ... Brough, P. (2019). Clean as a whistle: a five step guide to better whistleblowing policy and practice in business and government. *Whistling While They Work 2 – Key findings and actions*. Griffith University, Brisbane.

Brown, B. (2018). *Dare to lead: Brave work. Tough conversations. Whole hearts*. London: Random House.

Brown, K. W., Ryan, R. M., & Creswell, J. D. (2007). Mindfulness: Theoretical foundations and evidence for its salutary effects. *Psychological Inquiry, 18*(4), 211–237.

Burgess, M. G., Brough, P., Biggs, A., & Hawkes, A. J. (2020). Why interventions fail: A systematic review of occupational health psychology interventions. *International Journal of Stress Management, 27*(2), 195–207.

Burns, W. A. (2021). A typology of destructive leadership: Pseudo transformational, laissez-faire, and unethical causal factors and predictors. In S. M. Camgöz & Ö. T. Ekmekci (Eds.), *Destructive leadership and management hypocrisy* (pp. 49–66). Bingley: Emerald Publishing Limited.

Burton, H., Webster, V., & Lees, A. (2010). How to get ahead without murdering your boss: six simple steps to actively manage your career. NSW: A&A Publishing.

Burton, J. P., Hoobler, J. M., & Scheuer, M. L. (2012). Supervisor workplace stress and abusive supervision: The buffering effect of exercise. *Journal of Business Psychology, 27*, 271–279.

Burton, N. W., Pakenham, K. I., & Brown, W. J. (2010). Feasibility and effectiveness of psychosocial resilience training: A pilot study of the READY program. *Psychology, Health & Medicine, 15*(3), 266–277.

Byrne, A., Dionisi, A. M., Barling, J., Akers, A., Robertson, J., Lys, R., ... Dupré, K. (2014). The depleted leader: The influence of leaders' diminished psychological resources on leadership behaviors. *The Leadership Quarterly, 25*, 344–357.

Campbell, W. K., Hoffman, B. J., Campbell, S. M., & Marchisio, G. (2011). Narcissism in organizational contexts. *Human Resource Management Review, 21*, 268–284.

Carlson, D., Ferguson, M., Hunter, E., & Whitten, D. (2012). Abusive supervision and work–family conflict: The path through emotional labor and burnout. *The Leadership Quarterly, 23*(5), 849–859.

Catanzariti, J., & Egan, K. (2015). *Workplace bullying*. NSW: LexisNexis Butterworths.

Caza, A., & Jackson, B. (2011). Authentic leadership. In A. Bryman, D. Collinson, K. Grint, B. Jackson, & M. Uhl-Bien (Eds.), *The SAGE handbook of leadership* (pp. 352–364). Thousand Oaks, CA: Sage.

Chan, X. W., Shang, S., Brough, P., Wilkinson, A., & Lu, C. (2021, June). Work, life, and the COVID-19 pandemic (Working paper). Retrieved from www.griffith.edu.au/__data/assets/pdf_file/0023/1361750/Work,-Life,-and-the-COVID-19-Final.pdf

Chen, S. C., & Liu, N. T. (2019). When and how vicarious abusive supervision leads to bystanders' supervisor-directed deviance: A moderated–mediation model. *Personnel Review, 48*(7), 1734–1755.

Chi, S. C. S., & Liang, S. G. (2013). When do subordinates' emotion-regulation strategies matter? Abusive supervision, subordinates' emotional exhaustion, and work withdrawal. *The Leadership Quarterly, 24*(1), 125–137.

Chintakananda, K., & Greguras, G. (2017). Abusive supervision and power distance: Exploring discrete emotions. *Academy of Management Proceedings, 2017*(1), 16094.

Christiansen, N. D., Quirk, S. W., Robie, C., & Oswald, F. L. (2014). Light already defines the darkness: Understanding normal and maladaptive personality in the workplace. *Industrial and Organizational Psychology, 7*, 138–143.

Christie, R., & Geis, F. (1970). *Studies in Machiavellianism*. San Diego, CA: Academic Press.

Clarke, J. (2005). *Working with monsters. How to identify and protect yourself from the workplace psychopath*. Sydney: Random House.

Collins, M. D., & Jackson, C. J. (2015). A process model of self-regulation and leadership: How attentional resource capacity and negative emotions influence constructive and destructive leadership. *The Leadership Quarterly, 26*(3), 386–401.

Collis, R. (2013). *Applying ACT to workplace coaching. A guide to using acceptance and commitment training in work related coaching*. Retrieved from www.actmindfully.com.au/upimages/Applying_ACT_to_Workplace_Coaching_Rachel_Collis_ebook.pdf

Conger, J. A. (1990). The dark side of leadership. *Organizational Dynamics, 19*(2), 44–55.

Copeland, M. K. (2014). The emerging significance of values-based leadership: A literature review. *International Journal of Leadership Studies, 8*(2), 105–135.

Costa Jr, P. T., & McCrae, R. R. (1992). Four ways five factors are basic. *Personality and individual differences, 13*(6), 653–665.

Crawshaw, L. (2010). Coaching abrasive leaders: Using action research to reduce suffering and increase productivity in organizations. *The International Journal of Coaching in Organizations, 29*(8), 1, 60–77.

Crocker, J. (2002). Contingencies of self-worth: Implications for self-regulation and psychological vulnerability. *Self and Identity, 1*, 143–149.

Crowley, K., & Elster, K. (2009). *Working for you isn't working for me*. New York: Penguin Group.

Curtin, J. (2018). Innovative practices in workplace conflict resolution. In M. P. Duffy & D. C. Yamada (Eds.), *Workplace bullying and mobbing in the United States* (Part III), (Vol. 1, pp. 265–288). Santa Barbara: Praeger.

Dahling, J. J., Whitaker, B. G., & Levy, P. E. (2009). The development and validation of a new Machiavellianism scale. *Journal of Management, 35*(2), 219–257.

Daniel, T. A. (2017). Managing toxic emotions at work: HR's unique role as the 'organizational shock absorber'. *Employment Relations Today, 43*(4), 13–19.

Daniel, T. A. (2020). Organizational toxin handlers. *The critical role of HR, OD, and coaching practitioners in managing toxic workplace situations*. Cham, Switzerland: Palgrave Macmillan.

Day, D. V., Fleenor, J. W., Atwater, L. E., Sturm, R. E., & McKee, R. A. (2014). Advances in leader and leadership development: A review of 25 years of research and theory. *The Leadership Quarterly, 25*(1), 63–82.

De Fruyt, F., Wille, B., & Furnham, A. (2013). Assessing aberrant personality in managerial coaching: Measurement issues and prevalence rates across employment sectors. *European Journal of Personality, 27*, 555–564.

De Hoogh, A. H. B., & Den Hartog, D. N. (2008). Ethical and despotic leadership, relationships with leader's social responsiblity, top management team effectiveness and subordinates' optimism: A multi-method study. *The Leadership Quarterly, 19*, 297–311.

de Villiers, R. (2014). Book essay on 'The dark side of transformational leadership: A critical perspective'. *Journal of Business Research, 67*(12), 2512–2514.

Dekker, S. (2017). Just culture. *Restoring trust and accountability in your organization.* Aldershot, UK: CRC Press.

Dekker, S. W., & Breakey, H. (2016). 'Just culture': Improving safety by achieving substantive, procedural and restorative justice. *Safety Science, 85*, 187–193.

Dewe, P. (1994). EAPs and stress management. *Personnel Review, 23*(7), 21–32.

DeYoung, C. G., Weisberg, Y. J., Quilty, L. C., & Peterson, J. B. (2013). Unifying the aspects of the Big Five, the interpersonal circumplex, and trait affiliation. *Journal of Personality, 81*(5), 465–475.

Diller, S.J., Frey, D., & Jonas, E. (2020). Coach me if you can! Dark Triad clients, their effect on coaches, and how coaches deal with them. *Coaching: An International Journal of Theory, Research and Practice, 14*(2), 1–17.

Dolce, V., Vayre, E., Molino, M., & Ghislieri, C. (2020). Far away, so close? The role of destructive leadership in the job demands–resources and recovery model in emergency telework. *Social Sciences, 9*(11), 196–218.

Dollard, M., Shimazu, A., Bin Nordin, R., Brough, P., & Tuckey, M. (Eds.). (2014). *Psychosocial factors at work in the Asia Pacific.* London: Springer.

Duffy, M. K., Ganster, D., & Pagon, M. (2002). Social undermining in the workplace. *Academy of Management Journal, 45*, 331–351.

Dyne, L. V., Ang, S., & Botero, I. C. (2003). Conceptualizing employee silence and employee voice as multidimensional constructs. *Journal of Management Studies, 40*(6), 1359–1392.

Edgerton, N., & Palmer, S. (2005). SPACE: A psychological model for use within cognitive behavioural coaching, therapy and stress management. *The Coaching Psychologist, 1*(2), 25–31.

Einarsen, S., Aasland, M. S., & Skogstad, A. (2007). Destructive leadership behaviour: A definition and conceptual model. *The Leadership Quarterly, 18*, 207–216.

Einarsen, S., Skogstad, A., & Aasland, M. S. (2010). The nature, prevalence, and outcomes of destructive leadership – a behavioral and conglomerate approach. In B. Schyns & T. Hansborough (Eds.), *When leadership goes wrong: Destructive leadership, mistakes and ethical failures* (pp. 145–171). Chicago: Information Age Publishing.

Erickson, A., Shaw, B., Murray, J., & Branch, S. (2015). Destructive leadership: Causes, consequences and countermeasures. *Organizational Dynamics, 4*(44), 266–272.

Faldetta, G. (2019). When relationships are broken: Restorative justice under a Levinasian approach. *Philosophy of Management, 18*(1), 55–69.

Farh, C. I., & Chen, Z. (2014). Beyond the individual victim: Multilevel consequences of abusive supervision in teams. *Journal of Applied Psychology, 99*(6), 1074–1095.

Fatima, T., Majeed, M., & Jahanzeb, S. (2020). Supervisor undermining and submissive behavior: Shame resilience theory perspective. *European Management Journal, 38*(1), 191–203.

Fehr, R., & Gelfand, M. J. (2012). The forgiving organization: A multilevel model of forgiveness at work. *Academy of Management Review, 37*, 664–688.

Ferris, G. R., Zinko, R., Brouer, R. L., Buckley, M. R., & Harvey, M. G. (2007). Strategic bullying as a supplementary, balanced perspective on destructive leadership. *Leadership Quarterly, 18*, 195–206.

Feser, C., Nielsen, N., & Rennie, M. (2017). What's missing in leadership development? *McKinsey Quarterly, August*, 1–5.

Fitzgerald, M. (2006). *Corporate circles: Transforming conflict and building trusting teams.* Pennsylvania: Quinn Publishing.

Flaxman, P. E., & Bond, F. W. (2010a). A randomised worksite comparison of acceptance commitment therapy and stress inoculation training. *Behavior Research and Therapy, 48*, 816–820.

Flaxman, P. E., & Bond, F. W. (2010b). Worksite stress management training: Moderated effects and cli nical significance. *Journal of Occupational Health Psychology, 15*(4), 347–358.

Flaxman, P. E., Bond, F. W., & Livheim, F. (2013). *The mindful and effective employee: An acceptance and commitment therapy training manual for improving well-being and performance.* Oakland, CA: New Harbinger Publications.

Fletcher, J. K., & Kaufer, K. (2003). Shared leadership. Paradox and possibility. In C. L. Pearce & J. A. Conger (Eds.), *Shared leadership: Reframing the hows and whys of leadership* (pp. 21–47). California: Sage.

Ford, J., & Harding, N. (2011). The impossibility of the 'true self' of authentic leadership. *Leadership, 7*(4), 463–479.

Forst, G. (2013). Whistleblowing im internationalen Vergleich–Was kann Deutschland von seinen Nachbarn lernen. *Europäische Zeitschrift für Arbeitsrecht (EuZA), 6*, 37–82.

Fragouli, E. (2018). The dark-side of charisma and charismatic leadership. *Business and Management Review, 9*(4), 298–307.

Furnham, A., Richards, S.C., & Paulhus, D.L. (2013). The dark triad of personality: A 10 year review. *Social and Personality Psychology Compass, 7*(3), 199–216.

Furnham, A., Trickey, G., & Hyde, G. (2012). Bright aspects to dark side traits: Dark side traits associated with work success. *Personality and Individual Differences, 52*, 908–913.

Furtner, M. R., Maran, T., & Rauthmann, J. F. (2017). Dark leadership: The role of leaders' dark triad personality traits. In M. G. Clark & C. W. Gruber (Eds.), *Leader development deconstructed* (pp. 75–99). Cham: Springer.

Furtner, M. R., Rauthmann, J. F., & Sachse, P. (2011). The self-loving self-leader: an examination of the relationship between self-leadership and the dark triad. *Social Behavior and Personality: An International Journal, 39*(3), 369–379.

Gaddis, B. H., & Foster, J. L. (2015). Meta-analysis of dark side personality characteristics and critical work behaviors among leaders across the globe: Findings and implications for leadership development and executive coaching. *Applied Psychology: An International Review, 64*(1), 25–54.

Gallup (2020). *State of the American workplace report.* Washington: Gallup, Inc.

Gander, F., Proyer, R. T., Ruch, W., & Wyss, T. (2012). The good character at work: an initial study on the contribution of character strengths in identifying healthy and unhealthy work-related behaviour and experience patterns. *International Archives of Occupational and Environmental Health, 85*, 895–904.

Gentry, W. A., Hannum, K. M., Ekelund, B. Z., & de Jong, A. (2007). A study of the discrepancy between self- and observer-ratings on managerial derailment characteristics of European managers. *European Journal of Work and Organizational Psychology, 16*(30), 295–325.

Giga, S. I., Noblet, A. J., Faragher, B., & Cooper, C. L. (2003). The UK perspective: A review of research on organisational stress management interventions. *Australian Psychologist, 38*(2), 158–164.

Gilbreath, B., & Karimi, L. (2012). Supervisor behavior and employee presenteeism. *International Journal of Leadership Studies, 7*(1), 114–131.

Gkorezis, P., Petridou, E., & Krouklidou, T. (2015). The detrimental effect of Machiavellian leadership on employees' emotional exhaustion: Organizational cynicism as a mediator. *Europe's Journal of Psychology, 11*(4), 619–631.

Goh, U. W., Sawang, S., & Oei, T. P. S. (2010). The revised transactional model (RTM) of occupational stress and coping: An improved process approach. *The Australian and New Zealand Journal of Organisational Psychology, 3*, 13–20.

Gonzalez-Morales, M. G., Kernan, M. C., Becker, T. E., & Eisenberger, R. (2018). Defeating abusive supervision: Training supervisors to support subordinates. *Journal of Occupational Health Psychology, 23*(2), 151–172.

Goodstein, J., & Aquino, K. (2010). And restorative justice for all: Redemption, forgiveness, and reintegration in organizations. *Journal of Organizational Behavior, 31*(4), 624–628.

Greenberg, J. (1990). Organizational justice: Yesterday, today, and tomorrow. *Journal of Management, 16*(2), 399–432.

Grijalva, E., Harms, P. D., Newman, D. A., Gaddis, B. H., & Fraley, R. C. (2015). Narcissism and leadership: A meta-analytic review of linear and nonlinear relationships. *Personnel Psychology, 68*(1), 1–47.

Grijalva, E., & Newman, D. A. (2015). Narcissism and counterproductive work behaviour (CWB): Meta-analysis and consideration of collectivist culture, Big Five personality, and narcissism's facet structure. *Applied Psychology: An International Review, 64*(1), 93–126.

Gupta, R., Bakhshi, A., & Einarsen, S. (2017). Investigating workplace bullying in India: Psychometric properties, validity, and cutoff scores of negative acts questionnaire–revised. *Sage Open, 7*(2), 1–12.

Hannah, S. T., & Avolio, B. J. (2010). Moral potency: Building the capacity for character-based leadership. *Consulting Psychology Journal: Practice and Research, 62*(4), 291–310.

Hansbrough, T., & Schyns, B. (2010). Heroic Illusions. How implicit leadership theories shape follower attributions about poor leader performance. In B. Schyns &

T. Hansbrough (Eds.), *When leadership goes wrong. Destructive leadership, mistakes and ethical failures* (pp. 513–524). Charlotte, NC: Information Age Publishing, Inc.

Harms, P. D., Credé, M., Tynan, M., Leon, M., & Jeung, W. (2017). Leadership and stress: A meta-analytic review. *The Leadership Quarterly, 28*(1), 178–194.

Harms, P. D., Spain, S. M., & Hannah, S. T. (2011). Leader development and the dark side of personality. *The Leadership Quarterly, 22*, 495–509.

Harris, R. (2009). *The happiness trap. How to stop struggling and start living: A guide to ACT*. Boston: Trumpeter Books.

Harvey, P., Stoner, J., Hochwarter, W., & Kacmar, C. (2007). Coping with abusive supervision: The neutralizing effects of ingratiation and positive affect on negative employee outcomes. *Leadership Quarterly, 18*, 219–239.

Hawkes, A., & Spedding, J. (in press). Successful leadership. In Brough, P., Gardiner, E., & Daniels, K. (Eds). *Handbook on management and employment practices*. London: Springer.

He, Q., Wu, M., Wu, W., & Fu, J. (2021). The effect of abusive supervision on employees' work procrastination behavior. *Frontiers in Psychology, 12*, 113–125.

Heatherton, T. F., & Baumeister, R. F. (1996). Self-regulation failure: Past, present, and future. *Psychological Inquiry, 7*(1), 90–98.

Heppell, T. (2011). Toxic leadership: Applying the Lipman-Blumen model to political leadership. *Representation, 47*(3), 241–249.

Hernandez, M., & Sitkin, S. B. (2012). Who Is leading the leader? Follower influence on leader ethicality. In D. De Cremer & A. E. Tenbrunsel (Eds.), *Behavioral Business Ethics* (pp. 95–116). London: Routledge.

Higgins, E. T. (1987). Self-discrepancy: A theory relating self and affect. *Psychological Review, 94*(3), 319–340.

Higgins, E. T. (1997). Beyond pleasure and pain. *American Psychologist, 52*(12), 1280–1300.

Hobman, E. V., Restubog, S. L. D., Bordia, P., & Tang, R. L. (2009). Abusive supervision in advising relationships: Investigating the role of social support. *Applied Psychology: An International Review, 58*, 233–256.

Hoffren, M., & Laulainen, S. (2018). Destructive leadership as a wicked problem in health care: Can we blame the leader only? In W. Thomas, A. Hujala, S. Laulainen, & R. McMurray (Eds.), *The Management of Wicked Problems in Health and Social Care* (pp. 117–128). London: Routledge.

Hogan, R., Curphy, G. J., & Hogan, J. (1994). What we know about leadership: Effectiveness and personality. *American Psychologist, 49*, 493–504.

Hogan, R., & Hogan, J. (2001). Assessing leadership: A view from the dark side. *International Journal of Selection and Assessment, 9*(1/2), 40–51.

Hogan, R., Kaiser, R. B., Sherman, R. A., & Harms, P. D. (2021). Twenty years on the dark side: Six lessons about bad leadership. *Consulting Psychology Journal: Practice and Research, 73*(3), 199–213.

Hogan, R., Raskin, R., & Fazzini, D. (1990). The dark side of charisma. In K. E. Clark & M. B. Clark (Eds.), *Measures of leadership* (pp. 343–354). West Orange, NJ: Leadership Library of America.

Hogg, M. A., & Reid, S. A. (2001). Social identity, leadership, and power. In A. Y. Lee-Chai & J. A. Bargh (Eds.), *The use and abuse of power: Multiple perspectives on the causes of corruption* (p. 159–180). Psychology Press.

Holland, P. (2019). The impact of a dysfunctional leader on the workplace: a new challenge for HRM. *Personnel Review, 49*, 4, 1039–1052.

Hoobler, J. M., & Brass, D. J. (2006). Abusive supervision and family undermining as displaced aggression. *Journal of Applied Psychology, 91*(5), 1125–1133.

Hopkins, B. (2015). From restorative justice to restorative culture. *Social Work Review/Revista De Asistenta Sociala, 14*(4), 19–34.

House, R. J., & Howell, J. M. (1992). Personality and charismatic leadership. *Leadership Quarterly, 3*(2), 81–108.

Hu, L., & Liu, Y. (2017). Abuse for status: A social dominance perspective of abusive supervision. *Human Resource Management Review, 27*(2), 328–337.

Ibarra, H. (2015). The authenticity paradox. *Harvard Business Review, 93*(1/2), 53–59.

Jonason, P. K., & Webster, G. D. (2010). The dirty dozen: A concise measure of the dark triad. *Psychological Assessment, 22*(2), 420–432.

Jones, A., & Kelly, D. (2014). Deafening silence? Time to reconsider whether organisations are silent or deaf when things go wrong. *British Management Journal: Quality & Safety, 23*(9), 709–713.

Jordan, P. J., & Lindebaum, D. (2015). A model of within person variation in leadership: Emotion regulation and scripts as predictors of situationally appropriate leadership. *The Leadership Quarterly, 26*, 594–605.

Joseph, B., Walker, A., & Fuller-Tyszkiewicz, M. (2018). Evaluating the effectiveness of employee assistance programmes: A systematic review. *European Journal of Work and Organizational Psychology, 27*(1), 1–15.

Judge, T. A., & Bono, J. E. (2000). Five-factor model of personality and transformational leadership. *Journal of Applied Psychology, 85*, 751–765.

Judge, T. A., Bono, J. E., Illies, R., & Gerhardt, M. W. (2002). Personality and leadership: A qualitative and quantitative review. *Journal of Applied Psychology, 87*(4), 765–780.

Judge, T. A., & LePine, J. A. (2007). The bright and dark sides of personality: Implications for personnel selection in individual and team contexts. In J. Langan-Fox, C. L. Cooper, & R. J. Klimoski (Eds.), *Research companion to the dysfunctional workplace: Management challenges and symptoms.* (pp. 332–355). Cheltenham, UK: Edward Elgar Publishing Limited.

Judge, T. A., Piccolo, R. F., & Kosalka, T. (2009). The bright and dark sides of leader traits: A review and theoretical extension of the leader trait paradigm. *The Leadership Quarterly, 20*(6), 855–875.

Jülich, S., & Cox, N. (2013). Good workplaces: Alternative dispute resolution and restorative Justice. In J. Parker (Ed.), *The big issues in employment: HR management and employment relations in NZ* (pp. 1–26). Christchurch: CCH New Zealand.

Kaiser, R. B., & Hogan, J. (2011). Personality, leader behavior, and overdoing it. *Consulting Psychology Journal: Practice and Research, 63*(4), 219–242.

Kaiser, R. B., LeBreton, J. M., & Hogan, J. (2015). The dark side of personality and extreme leader behavior. *Applied Psychology: An International Review, 64*(1), 55–92.

Kaptein, M. (2011). Understanding unethical behavior by unraveling ethical culture. *Human Relations, 64*(6), 843–869.

Karoly, P. (1993). Mechanisms of self-regulation: A systems view. *Annual Review Psychology, 44*, 23–52.

Karp, D. R. (2019). *The little book of restorative justice for colleges and universities: Repairing harm and rebuilding trust in response to student misconduct*. New York: Simon and Schuster.

Kaufman, S. B., Yaden, D. B., Hyde, E., & Tsukayama, E. (2019). The light vs. dark triad of personality: Contrasting two very different profiles of human nature. *Frontiers in Psychology, 10*, Article 467, 1–26.

Kellerman, B. (2004). *Bad leadership: What it is, how it happens, why it matters*. New York: Harvard Business Review Press.

Kellerman, B. (2008). *Followership: How followers are creating change and changing leaders*. Boston: Harvard Business School Publishing.

Keng, F. T., Feng, Z., & Li, H. (2018). How Machiavellian leaders strategically use abusive supervision to overpower their subordinates. *Academy of Management Proceedings, 2018*(1), 16410.

Khoo, H., & Burch, G. (2008). The 'dark side' of leadership personality and transformational leadership. *Personality and Individual Differences, 44*, 86–97.

Kidd, J. M. (2008). Exploring the components of career well-being and the emotions associated with significant career experiences. *Journal of Career Development, 35*(2), 166–186.

Kiewitz, C., Restubog, S. L. D., Shoss, M. K., Garcia, P. R. J. M., & Tang, R. L. (2016). Suffering in silence: Investigating the role of fear in the relationship between abusive supervision and defensive silence. *Journal of Applied Psychology, 101*, 731–742.

Kilmann, R. H., O'Hara, L. A., & Strauss, J. P. (2013). Developing and validating a quantitative measure of organizational courage. In R. J. Burke & C. Cooper (Eds.), *Voice and whistleblowing in organizations* (pp. 311–342). Cheltenham: Edward Elgar.

Kim, J. K., Holtz, B. C., & Hu, B. (2020). Rising above: Investigating employee exemplification as a response to the experience of shame induced by abusive supervision. *Journal of Occupational and Organizational Psychology, 93*(4), 861–886.

King, G. A., & Rothstein, M. G. (2010). Resilience and leadership: The self-management of failure. In M. G. Rothstein & R. J. Burke (Eds.), *Self-management and leadership development* (pp. 361–394). Cheltenham: Edward Elgar Publishing.

Kouzes, J., & Posner, B. (2015). *Extraordinary Leadership in Australia and New Zealand: The Five Practices that Create Great Workplaces*. Melbourne: John Wiley & Sons Australia, Ltd.

Krasikova, D. V., Green, S. G., & LeBreton, J. M. (2013). Destructive leadership: A theoretical review, integration, and future research agenda. *Journal of Management, 39*(5), 1308–1338.

Labrague, L. J., Nwafor, C. E., & Tsaras, K. (2020). Influence of toxic and transformational leadership practices on nurses' job satisfaction, job stress, absenteeism and turnover intention: A cross-sectional study. *Journal of Nursing Management, 28*(5), 1104–1113.

Lamontagne, A. D., Keegel, T., Louie, A. M., Ostry, A., & Landsbergis, P. A. (2007). A systematic review of the job-stress intervention evaluation literature, 1990–2005. *International Journal of Occupational and Environmental Health, 13*(3), 268–280.

Lawrence, P. (2019). What is systemic coaching? *Philosophy of Coaching: An International Journal, 4*(2), November, 35–52.

Lawrence, S. A., Troth, A. C., Jordan, P. J., & Collins, A. L. (2011). A review of emotion regulation and development of a framework for emotion regulation in the workplace. In P. L. Perrewé & D. C. Ganster (Eds.), *The role of individual differences in occupational stress and well being* (pp. 197–263). Bingley, UK: Emerald Group Publishing Limited.

Lazarus, R. (1966). *Psychological stress and the coping process.* New York: McGraw-Hill.

Leary, T., & Ashman, J. (2018). Narcissistic leadership: Important considerations and practical implications. *International Leadership Journal, 10*(2), 62–74.

Lencioni, P. (2006). *The five dysfunctions of a team.* San Francisco: John Wiley & Sons.

Leslie, J. B., & Velsor, E. V. (1996). *A look at derailment today: North America and Europe.* Greensborough, NC: CCL Press.

Lian, H., Brown, D. J., Ferris, D. L., Liang, L. H., Keeping, L. M., & Morrison, R. (2014). Abusive supervision and retaliation: A self-control framework. *Academy of Management Journal, 57*(1), 116–139.

Lian, H., Ferris, D. L., & Brown, D. J. (2012). Does power distance exacerbate or mitigate the effects of abusive supervision? It depends on the outcome. *Journal of Applied Psychology, 97*(1), 107–123.

Liebmann, M. (2007). *Restorative justice. How it works.* Philidelphia: Jessica Kingsley Publishers.

Lilienfield, S. O., & Andrews, B. P. (1996). Development and preliminary validation of a self-report measure of psychopathic personality traits in noncriminal populations. *Journal of Personality Assessment, 66*(3), 488–524.

Lin, S. H., Scott, B. A., & Matta, F. K. (2019). The dark side of transformational leader behaviors for leaders themselves: A conservation of resources perspective. *Academy of Management Journal, 62*(5), 1556–1582.

Lincoln, K. D. (2000). Social support, negative social interactions, and psychological well-being. *Social Service Review, 74*(2), 231–252.

Lipman-Blumen, J. (2005). *The allure of toxic leaders: Why we follow destructive bosses and corrupt politicians - and how we can survive them.* Oxford: Oxford University Press.

Locke, C. C., & Anderson, C. (2015). The downside of looking like a leader: Power, nonverbal confidence, and participative decision-making. *Journal of Experimental Social Psychology, 58*, 42–47.

London, M. (1997). Overcoming career barriers: A model of cognitive and emotional processes for realistic appraisal and constructive coping. *Journal of Career Development, 24*(1), 25–28.

Lopes, B. C., Kamau, C., & Jaspal, R. (2019). Coping with perceived abusive supervision: the role of paranoia. *Journal of Leadership & Organizational Studies, 26*(2), 237–255.

Lubit, R. H. (2004). *Coping with toxic managers, subordinates and other difficult people.* Upper Saddle River, NJ: Pearson Education Inc.

Maccoby, M. (2007). *Narcisstic leaders: Who succeeds and who fails.* New York: Harvard Business School Press.

Maner, J. K., & Mead, N.L. (2010). The essential tension between leadership and power: When leaders sacrifice group goals for the sake of self-interest. *Journal of Personality and Social Psychology, 99*, 482–497.

Martinko, M. J., Harvey, P., Brees, J. R., & Mackey, J. (2013). A review of abusive supervision research. *Journal of Organizational Behavior, 34*, S120–S137.

Mathieu, C., & Babiak, P. (2016). Corporate psychopathy and abusive supervision: Their influence on employees' job satisfaction and turnover intentions. *Personality and Individual Differences, 91*, 102–106.

Mathur, G., & Chauhan, A. S. (2018). Analyzing the relationship between depression, abusive supervision & organizational deviance: an SEM approach. *Journal of Human Resource Management, 21*(1), 1–13.

Matos, K., O'Neill, O., & Lei, X. (2018). Toxic leadership and the masculinity contest culture: How 'win or die' cultures breed abusive leadership. *Journal of Social Issues, 74*(3), 500–528.

Mawritz, M. B., Folger, R., & Lathan, G. P. (2014). Supervisors' exceedingly difficult goals and abusive supervision: The mediating effects of hindrance stress, anger, and anxiety. *Journal of Organizational Behavior, 35*, 358–372.

May, D., Wesche, J. S., Heinitz, K., & Kerschreiter, R. (2014). Coping with destructive leadership. Putting forward an integrated theoretical framework for the interaction process between leaders and followers. *Journal of Psychology, 222*(4), 203–213.

McCall, M. W. J., & Lombardo, M. M. (1983). *Off the track: Why and how successful executives get derailed* (Leadership Report no. 21). Greensboro: Center for Creative Leadership.

McClelland, D. C. (1970). The two faces of power. *Journal of International Affairs, 24*, 29–47.

McClelland, D. C. (1975). *Power: The inner experience.* New York: Irvington.

McClelland, D. C. (1985). How motives, skills, and values determine what people do. *American Psychologist, 40*(7), 812–825.

McClelland, D. C. (1992). Motivational configurations. In C. P. Smith (Ed.), *Motivation and personality: Handbook of thematic content analysis* (pp. 87–99). New York: Cambridge University Press.

McClelland, D. C., & Boyatzis, R. E. (1982). Leadership motive pattern and long-term success in management. *Journal of Applied Psychology, 67*, 737–743.

McEwen, K. (2016). Building your resilience. How to thrive in a challenging job. *Working With Resilience.* Retrieved from https://workingwithresilience.com.au/

McFarlin, D. B., & Sweeney, P. D. (2010). The corporate reflecting pool - antecedents and consequences of narcissism in executives. In B. Schyns & T. Hansborough (Eds.), *When leadership goes wrong: Destructive leadership, mistakes and ethical failures* (pp. 247–283). Chicago: Information Age Publishing.

McLarnon, M. J. W., & Rothstein, M. G. (2013). Development and initial validation of the Workplace Resilience Inventory. *Journal of Personnel Psychology, 12*(2), 63–73.

McNeill, S. (2020). *We can't say we didn't know. Dispatches from an age of impunity.* Sydney: Harper Collins.

Medina, A., Lopez, E., & Medina, R. (2020). The unethical managerial behaviours and abusive use of power in downwards vertical workplace bullying: a phenomenological case study. *Social Sciences, 9*(6), 110–125.

Mehta, S., & Maheshwari, G. C. (2013). Consequence of toxic leadership on employee job satisfaction and organizational commitment. *Journal of Contemporary Management Research, 7* (2) 1–23.

Meichenbaum, D. (1996). Stress inoculation training for coping with stressors. *The Clinical Psychologist, 49*, 4–7.

Meichenbaum, D. (2017). Stress inoculation training. In D. Meichenbaum (Ed.), *The evolution of Cognitive Behavior Therapy: A personal and professional journey with Don Meichenbaum* (pp. 101–124). New York: Routledge.

Meyer, K. (2011). Restorative circles: Past, present, and future. *Conflict Resolution & Negotiation Journal, March*(1), 88–93.

Meyers, M. C., van Woerkom, M., & Bakker, A. B. (2013). The added value of the positive: A literature review of positive psychology interventions in organizations. *European Journal of Work and Organizational Psychology, 22*(5), 618–632.

Miceli, M. P., & Near, J. P. (2013). An international comparison of the incidence of public sector whistle-blowing and the prediction of retaliation: Australia, Norway, and the US. *Australian Journal of Public Administration, 72*(4), 433–446.

Michel, J. S., Newness, K., & Duniewicz, K. (2016). How abusive supervision affects workplace deviance: A moderated-mediation examination of aggressiveness and work-related negative affect. *Journal of Business and Psychology, 31*(1), 1–22.

Milosevic, I., Maric, S., & Lončar, D. (2020). Defeating the toxic boss: The nature of toxic leadership and the role of followers. *Journal of Leadership & Organizational Studies, 27*(2), 117–137.

Mitchell, M. S., & Ambrose, M. L. (2007). Abusive supervision and workplace deviance and the moderating effects of negative reciprocity beliefs. *Journal of Applied Psychology, 92*(4), 1159–1168.

Mitchell, M. S., & Ambrose, M. L. (2012). Employees' behavioral reactions to supervisor aggression: An examination of individual and situational factors. *Journal of Applied Ppsychology, 97*(6), 1148–1170.

Mitchell, M. S., Vogel, R. M., & Folger, R. (2015). Third parties' reactions to the abusive supervision of coworkers. *Journal of Applied Psychology, 100*, 1040–1055.

Molino, M., Cortese, C. G., & Ghislieri, C. (2019). Unsustainable working conditions: The association of destructive leadership, use of technology, and workload with workaholism and exhaustion. *Sustainability, 11*(2), 446–460.

Moore, D. B. (1996). *Transformation in the workplace: Affect and script in the business world*. Central Tablelands and Blue Mountains Community: Transformative Justice Australia.

Moore, D. B. (1998). Justice in the workplace: The transformation of economic communities. *Humanity & Society, 22*(1), 79–97.

Moore, D. B. (2004). Managing social conflict - The evolution of a practical theory. *Journal of Sociology and Social Welfare, 31*, 71–91.

Moran, D. J. (2011). ACT for leadership: Using acceptance and commitment training to develop crisis-resilient change managers. *The International Journal of Behavioral Consultation and Therapy, 7*(1), 68–77.

Moran, D. J. (2015). Acceptance and commitment training in the workplace. *Current Opinion in Psychology, 2*, 26–31.

Morrison, E. W. (2014). Employee voice and silence. *Annual Review of Organizational Psychology & Organizational Behavior, 1*(1), 173–197.

Morrison, E. W., & Milliken, F. J. (2000). Organizational silence: A barrier to change and development in a pluralistic world. *Academy of Management Review, 25*(4), 706–725.

Mulvey, P. W., & Padilla, A. (2010). The environment of destructive leadership. In B. Schyns & T. Hansborough (Eds.), *When leadership goes wrong: Destructive leadership, mistakes and ethical failures* (pp. 49–71). Chicago: Information Age Publishing.

Nafei, W. A. (2016). Organizational silence: a barrier to job engagement in successful organizations. *International Business Research, 9*(4), 100–117.

Nandkeolyar, A. K., Shaffer, J. A., Li, A., Ekkirala, S., & Bagger, J. (2014). Surviving an abusive supervisor: The joint roles of conscientiousness and coping strategies. *Journal of Applied Psychology, 99*(1), 138–150.

Neenan, M., & Palmer, S. (2006). Cognitive behavioural coaching. In J. Passmore (Ed.), *Excellence in coaching: The industry guide* (pp. 91–105). London: Kogan Page Limited.

Nelson, E., & Hogan, R. (2009). Coaching on the dark side. *International Coaching Psychology Review, 4*(1), 7–19.

Nielsen, K., Taris, T. W., & Cox, T. (2010). The future of organizational interventions: Addressing the challenges of today's organizations. *Work & Stress: An International Journal of Work, Health & Organisations, 24*(3), 219–233.

Nyberg, D., & Sveningsson, S. (2014). Paradoxes of authentic leadership: Leader identity struggles. *Leadership, 10*(4), 437–455.

O'Boyle, E. H., & Forsyth, D. R. (2012). A meta-analysis of the dark triad and work behavior: A social exchange perspective. *Journal of Applied Psychology, 97*(3), 557–579.

O'Driscoll, M. P., & Brough, P. (2010). Work organization and health. In S. Leka & J. Houdmont (Eds.), *Occupational Health Psychology* (pp. 57–87). Chichester: Wiley-Blackwell.

O'Driscoll, M., Brough, P., & Kalliath, T. (2009). Stress and coping. In S. Cartwright & C. L. Cooper (Eds.), *The Oxford handbook of organizational well being* (pp. 237–266). Oxford: Oxford University Press.

Okimoto, T. G., & Wenzel, M. (2014). Bridging diverging perspectives and repairing damaged relationships in the aftermath of workplace transgressions. *Business Ethics Quarterly, 24*(3), 443–473.

O'Sullivan, M. (2017). The structural causes of workplace conflict: Understanding the implications for the mediation of workplace disputes. *Bond Law Review, 29*, 87–94.

Padilla, A., Hogan, R., & Kaiser, R. B. (2007). The toxic triangle: Destructive leaders, susceptible followers and conducive environments. *The Leadership Quarterly, 18*, 176–194.

Paul, G. D. (2017). Paradoxes of restorative justice in the workplace. *Management Communication Quarterly, 31*(3), 380–408.

PBC Hogan (2020). *PBC Hogan handbook: An abridged guide to interpreting and using the HPI, HDS and MVPI*. Sydney: Peter Berry Consultancy Pty Ltd.

Pelletier, K. L. (2010). Leader toxicity: An empirical investigation of toxic behaviour and rhetoric. *Leadership, 6*(4), 373–389.

Peng, A. C., M. Schaubroeck, J., Chong, S., & Li, Y. (2019). Discrete emotions linking abusive supervision to employee intention and behavior. *Personnel Psychology, 72*(3), 393–419.

Pipe, T. B., Buchda, V. L., Launder, S., Hudak, B., Hulvey, L., Karns, K. E., & Pendergast, D. (2012). Building personal and professional resources of resilience and agility in the healthcare workplace. *Stress and Health, 28*, 11–22.

Plate, M. (2015). Shame and the undoing of leadership – An analysis of shame in organizations. In C. E. Hartel, W. J. Zerbe, & N. M. Ashkanasy (Eds.), *New ways of studying emotions in organizations. Research on emotion in organizations* (Vol. 11, pp. 81–107). Bingley: Emerald Group Publishing Limited.

Pope, R. (2019). Organizational silence in the NHS: 'Hear no, see no, speak no'. *Journal of Change Management, 19*(1), 45–66.

Price Waterhouse Coopers. (2014). Creating a mentally health workplace: Return on investment analysis. *Beyond Blue*. Retrieved from www.headsup.org.au.

Priesemuth, M. (2013). Stand up and speak up: Employees' prosocial reactions to observed abusive supervision. *Business & Society, 52*(4), 649–665.

Priesemuth, M., & Schminke, M. (2019). Helping thy neighbor? Prosocial reactions to observed abusive supervision in the workplace. *Journal of Management, 45*(3), 1225–1251.

Pundt, A. (2014). A multiple pathway model linking charismatic leadership attempts and abusive supervision. *Zeitschrift fur Psychologie, 222*, 190–202.

Pyc, L. S., Meltzer, D. P., & Liu, C. (2017). Ineffective leadership and employees' negative outcomes: The mediating effect of anxiety and depression. *International Journal of Stress Management, 24*(2), 196–215.

Quick, J. C., & Wright, T. A. (2011). Character-based leadership, context and consequences. *The Leadership Quarterly, 22*(5), 984–988.

Rafferty, A. E., & Restubog, S. L. D. (2011). The influence of abusive supervisors on followers' organizational citizenship behaviours: The hidden costs of abusive supervision. *British Journal of Management, 22*, 270–285.

Rai, A., & Agarwal, U. A. (2018). Workplace bullying and employee silence. *Personnel Review, 47*(1), 226–256.

Raper, M. J., & Brough, P. (2021). Seeing into the future: The role of future-oriented coping and daily stress appraisal in relation to a future stressor. *Stress and Health, 37*(1), 186–197.

Rawski, S. L., & Workman-Stark, A. L. (2018). Masculinity contest cultures in policing organizations and recommendations for training interventions. *Journal of Social Issues, 74*(3), 607–627.

Redeker, M., de Vries, R. E., Rouckhout, D., Vermeren, P., & de Fruyt, F. (2014). Integrating leadership: The leadership circumplex. *European Journal of Work and Organizational Psychology, 23*(3), 435–455.

Restubog, S. L. D., Scott, K. L., & Zagenczyk, T. J. (2011). When distress hits home: The role of contextual factors and psychological distress in predicting employees' responses to abusive supervision. *Journal of Applied Psychology, 96*(4), 713–729.

Richard, O. C., Boncoeur, O. D., Chen, H., & Ford, D. L. (2020). Supervisor abuse effects on subordinate turnover intentions and subsequent interpersonal aggression: The role of power-distance orientation and perceived human resource support climate. *Journal of Business Ethics, 164*(3), 549–563.

Richardson, K. M., & Rothstein, H. R. (2008). Effects of occupational stress manage-ment intervention programs: A meta-analysis. *Journal of Occupational and Health Psychology, 13*(1), 69–93.

Rogelberg, S. G., Justice, L., Braddy, P. W., Paustian-Underdahl, S. C., Heggestad, E., Shanock, L., ... Fleenor, J. W. (2013). The executive mind: leader self-talk, effec-tiveness and strain. *Journal of Managerial Psychology, 28*(2), 183–201.

Rosenthal, S. A., & Pittinsky, T. L. (2006). Narcissistic leadership. *The Leadership Quarterly, 17*, 617–633.

Ruderman, M. N., Hannum, K., Leslie, J. B., & Steed, J. L. (2001). Making the con-nection: leadership skills and emotional intelligence. *LIA, 21*(5), 3–7.

Safe Work Australia (2013). *The incidence of accepted workers' compensation claims for mental stress in Australia.* Canberra: Safe Work Australia.

Safe Work Australia (2015). *Key work health and safety statistics, Australia, 2015.* Canberra: Safe Work Australia.

Sandler, C. (2012). The emotional profiles triangle: Working with leaders under pressure. *Strategic HR Review, 11*(2), 65–71.

Saunders, T., Driskell, J. E., Johnston, J. H., & Salas, E. (1996). The effect of stress inoculation training on anxiety and performance. *Journal of Occupational Health Psychology, 1*(2), 170–186.

Schaufeli, W. B., Leiter, M. P., & Maslach, C. (2009). Burnout: 35 years of research and practice. *Career Development International, 14*(3), 204–220.

Schmid, E. A., Pircher Verdorfer, A., & Peus, C. V. (2018). Different shades—different effects? Consequences of different types of destructive leadership. *Frontiers in Psychology, 9*, Article 1289, 1–16.

Schmid, E. A., Pircher Verdorfer, A., & Peus, C. (2019). Shedding light on lead-ers' self-interest: theory and measurement of exploitative leadership. *Journal of Management, 45*(4), 1401–1433.

Schmit, M. J., Kihm, J. A., & Robie, C. (2000). Development of a global measure of personality. *Personnel Psychology, 53*(1), 153–193.

Schwartz, M. S. (2016). Ethical decision-making theory: An integrated approach. *Journal of Business Ethics, 139*(4), 755–776.

Schyns, B., & Hansborough, T. (2010). *When leadership goes wrong: Destructive lead-ership, mistakes and ethical failures.* Charlotte, NC: Information Age Publishing.

Schyns, B., & Schilling, J. (2013). How bad are the effects of bad leaders? A meta-analysis of destructive leadership and its outcomes. *The Leadership Quarterly, 24*, 138–158.

Scott, S. (2002). *Fierce conversations: Achieving success at work & in life, one conversa-tion at a time.* London: Penguin.

Seligman, M., & Csikszentmihalyi, M. (2000). Positive psychology: An introduction. *American Psychologist, 55*, 5–14.

Selye, H. (1956). *The stress of life.* New York: McGraw-Hill.

Selye, H. (1976). *Stress in health and disease.* London: Butterworths.

Shaw, J. B., Erickson, A., & Harvey, M. (2011). A method for measuring destruc-tive leadership and identifying types of destructive leaders in organizations. *The Leadership Quarterly, 22*, 4, 575–590.

Skinner, E. A., Edge, K., Altman, J., & Sherwood, H. (2003). Searching for the struc-ture of coping: a review and critique of category systems for classifying ways of coping. *Psychological Bulletin, 129*(2), 216–269.

Skogstad, A., Einarsen, S., Torsheim, T., Aasland, M. S., & Hetland, H. (2007). The destructiveness of laissez-faire leadership behaviour. *Journal of Occupational and Health Psychology, 12*(1), 80–92.

Smith, S. F., & Lilienfeld, S. O. (2013). Psychopathy in the workplace: The knowns and unknowns. *Aggression and Violent Behavior, 18*, 204–218.

Song, B., Qian, J., Wang, B., Yang, M., & Zhai, A. (2017). Are you hiding from your boss? Leader's destructive personality and employee silence. *Social Behavior and Personality: An International Journal, 45*(7), 1167–1174.

Spangler, W. D., Tikhomirov, A., Sotak, K. L., & Palrecha, R. (2014). Leader motive profiles in eight types of organizations. *The Leadership Quarterly, 25*(5), 1080–1094.

Sparks, K., Faragher, B., & Cooper, C. L. (2001). Well-being and occupational health in the 21st century workplace. *Journal of Occupational and Organizational Psychology, 74*, 489–509.

Spreier, S. W., Fontaine, M. H., & Malloy, R. L. (2006). Leadership run amok: The destructive potential of overachievers. *Harvard Business Review, June 2006*, 73–82.

Steinmann, B., Kleinert, A., & Maier, G. W. (2020). Promoting the underestimated: A vignette study on the importance of the need for affiliation to successful leadership. *Motivation and Emotion, 44*, 641–656.

Sutton, R. (2007). The no asshole rule. *Building a civilized workplace and surviving one that isn't*. New York: Business Plus.

TalentQ. (2013). *Dimensions psychometric review*. Philadelphia: Hay Group.

Tepper, B. J. (2000). Consequences of abusive supervision. *Academy of Management, 43*, 178–190.

Tepper, B. J. (2007). Abusive supervision in work organisations: Review, synthesis, and research agenda. *Journal of Management Development, 33*(3), 261–289.

Tepper, B. J., Carr, J. C., Breaux, D. M., Geider, S., Hu, C., & Hua, W. (2009). Abusive supervision, intentions to quit, and employees' workplace deviance: A power/dependence analysis. *Organizational Behavior and Human Decision Processes, 109*(2), 156–167.

Tepper, B. J., Duffy, M. K., Henle, C. A., & Lambert, L. S. (2006). Procedural injustice, victim precipitation, and abusive supervision. *Personnel Psychology, 59*, 101–123.

Tepper, B. J., Henle, C. A., Lambert, L. S., Giacalone, R. A., & Duffy, M. K. (2008). Abusive supervision and subordinates' organization deviance. *Journal of Applied Psychology, 93*(4), 721–732.

Tepper, B. J., Moss, S. E., Lockhart, D. E., & Carr, J. C. (2007). Abusive supervision, upward maintainance communication, and subordinates' psychological distress. *Academy of Management Journal, 50*(5), 1169–1180.

Tepper, B. J., Simon, L., & Park, H. M. (2017). Abusive supervision. *Annual Review of Organizational Psychology and Organizational Behavior, 4*, 123–152.

Thoroughgood, C. N., Padilla, A., Hunter, S. T., & Tate, B. W. (2012). The susceptible circle: A taxonomy of followers associated with destructive leadership. *The Leadership Quarterly, 23*, 897–917.

Thorsborne, M. (2014). *Workplace conferencing: A restorative approach to transforming workplace conflict*. Sunshine Coast: Margaret Thorsborne and Associates. Retrieved from www.thorsborne.com.au/training-manual/

Thorsborne, M. (2021). Case studies. Retrieved from www.thorsborne.com.au.

Tierney, P., & Tepper, B. J. (2007). Introduction to *The Leadership Quarterly* special issue: Destructive leadership (Editorial). *Leadership Quarterly, 18*(3), 171–173.

Tourish, D. (2013). *The dark side of transformational leadership: A critical perspective.* London: Routledge.

Trapnell, P. D., & Wiggins, J. S. (1990). Extension of the interpersonal adjective scales to include the big five dimensions of personality. *Journal of Personality and Social Psychology, 59*, 781–790.

Trickey, G., & Hyde, G. (2009). *A decade of the dark side. Fighting our demons at work.* White Paper. Tunbridge Wells, UK: Psychological Consultancy Limited.

Tsui, A. S., & Ashford, S. J. (1994). Adaptive self-regulation: A process view of managerial effectiveness. *Journal of Management, 20*(1), 93–121.

Ugaddan, R. G., & Park, S. M. (2019). Do trustful leadership, organizational justice, and motivation influence whistle-blowing intention? Evidence from federal employees. *Public Personnel Management, 48*(1), 56–81.

Uhl-Bien, M., Riggio, R. E., Lowe, K. B., & Carsten, M. K. (2014). Followership theory: A review and research agenda. *The Leadership Quarterly, 25*, 83–104.

van der Klink, J. J. L., Blonk, W. B. R., Schene, A. H., & van Dijk, F. J. H. (2001). The benefits of interventions for work-related stress. *American Journal of Public Health, 91*, 270–276.

van Emmerik, I. H., Euwema, M. C., & Bakker, A. B. (2007). Threats of workplace violence and the buffering effect of social support. *Group and Organization Management, 32*(2), 152–175.

van Knippenberg, D. (2012). Leadership: A person-in-situation perspective. In K. Deaux & M. Snyder (Eds.), *The Oxford handbook of personality and social psychology* (pp. 673–700). Oxford: Oxford University Press.

Victor, B., & Cullen, J. B. (1988). The organizational bases of ethical work climates. *Administrative Science Quarterly, 33*(1), 101–125.

Vullinghs, J. T., De Hoogh, A. H., Den Hartog, D. N., & Boon, C. (2020). Ethical and passive leadership and their joint relationships with burnout via role clarity and role overload. *Journal of Business Ethics, 165*(4), 719–733.

Vuori, J., Toppinen-Tanner, S., & Mutanen, P. (2012). Effects of resource-building group intervention on career management and mental health in work organisations: Randomised controlled field trial. *Journal of Applied Psychology, 97*(2), 273–286.

Wang, M., Sinclair, R., & Deese, M. N. (2010). Understanding the causes of destructive leadership behaviour - a dual-process model. In B. Schyns & T. Hansborough (Eds.), *When leadership goes wrong: Destructive leadership, mistakes and ethical failures* (pp. 73–97). Chicago: Information Age Publishing.

Watson, D., & Clark, L. A. (1984). Negative affectivity: the disposition to experience aversive emotional states. *Psychological Bulletin, 96*(3), 465–490.

Webster, V. (2016). *The dark side of leadership and its impact on followers* (dissertation), Griffith University, Australia.

Webster, V., & Brough, P. (2015). Assisting organisations to deal effectively with toxic leadership in the workplace. *InPsych: Bulletin of the Australian Psychological Society, June*, 24–25.

Webster, V., Brough, P., & Daly, K. (2016). Fight, flight or freeze: Common responses for follower coping with toxic leadership. *Stress & Health, 32*, 346–354.

Whitman, M. V., Halbesleben, J. R. B., & Shanine, K. K. (2013). Psychological entitlement and abusive supervision: Political skill as a self-regulatory mechanism. *Health Care Management Review, 38*(3), 248–257.

Williams, F. I., Campbell, C., McCartney, W., & Gooding, C. (2013). Leader derailment: the impact of self-defeating behaviors. *Leadership & Organization Development Journal, 34*(1), 85–97.

Winn, G. L., & Dykes, A. C. (2019). Identifying toxic leadership and building worker resilience. *Professional Safety, 64*(3), 38–45.

Wortley, R., Cassematis, P., & Donkin, M. (2008). Who blows the whistle, who doesn't and why. In A. J. Brown (Ed.), *Whistleblowing in the Australian public sector* (pp. 53–82). Canberra: ANU Press.

Wotruba, T. R., Chonko, L. B., & Loe, T. W. (2001). The impact of ethics code familiarity on manager behaviour. *Journal of Business Ethics, 33*(1), 59–69.

Wu, T. Y., & Hu, C. (2009). Abusive supervision and employee emotional exhaustion: Dispositional antecedents and boundaries. *Group and Organisation Management, 34*, 143–169.

Xu, A. J., Loi, R., & Lam, L. W. (2015). The bad boss takes it all: How abusive supervision and leader–member exchange interact to influence employee silence. *The Leadership Quarterly, 26*(5), 763–774.

Yagil, D., Ben-Zur, H., & Tamir, I. (2011). Do employees cope effectively with abusive supervision at work? An exploratory study. *International Journal of Stress Management, 18*(1), 5–23.

Zellars, K. L., Justice, L., & Beck, T. E. (2011). Resilience: New paths for building and sustaining individual and organizational capacity. *Research in Occupational Stress and Well Being, 9*, 1–37.

Zhang, Y., Liu, X., Xu, S., Yang, L. Q., & Bednall, T. C. (2019). Why abusive supervision impacts employee OCB and CWB: A meta-analytic review of competing mediating mechanisms. *Journal of Management, 45*(6), 2474–2497.

Zhou, L., Liu, Y., Chen, Z., & Zhao, S. (2018). Psychological mechanisms linking ethical climate to employee whistle-blowing intention. *Journal of Managerial Psychology, 33*(2), 196–213.

Zimmerman, B. J. (2000). Attaining self-regulation: A social cognitive perspective. In M. Boekaerts, P. R. Pintrich, & M. Zeidner (Eds.), *Self-regulation: Directions and challenges for future research* (pp. 12–40). New York: Academic Press.

INDEX

Ingram Content Group UK Ltd.
Milton Keynes UK
UKHW022228190423
420449UK00005B/127